The Social Work Ethics Audit

A Risk Management Tool

FREDERIC G. REAMER

NASW PRESS

National Association of Social Workers
Washington, DC

Ruth W. Mayden, MSS, LSW, ACSW, President
Toby Weismiller, ACSW, Interim Executive Director

D1323375

Library of Congress Cataloging-in-Publication Data

Reamer, Frederic G., 1953–
The social work ethics audit: A risk management tool / by Frederic G. Reamer.
    p. cm.
    Includes bibliographical references and index.
    ISBN 0-87101-328-2
    1. Social service--Moral and ethical aspects--Auditing. 2. Social workers--Professional ethics. I. Title.

    HV10.5 .R425 2001
    361.3'068'4—dc21

2001030021

CONTENTS

ABOUT THE AUTHOR

Frederic G. Reamer, PhD, is professor at the School of Social Work, Rhode Island College. Dr. Reamer has served as a social worker in mental health, correctional, and housing agencies, and in a governor's office. He was chair of the NASW *Code of Ethics* Revision Committee, and he lectures nationally and internationally on the subjects of social work and professional ethics. Dr. Reamer frequently consults with social workers and social service agencies concerning the issues addressed in *The Social Work Ethics Audit*. His other books include *Social Work Values and Ethics, Ethical Dilemmas in Social Service, Social Work Malpractice and Liability, The Philosophical Foundations of Social Work, The Foundations of Social Work Knowledge, AIDS and Ethics, Rehabilitating Juvenile Justice* (with Charles Shireman), *Social Work Research and Evaluation Skills, Ethical Standards in Social Work: A Review of the NASW Code of Ethics, Tangled Relationships: Managing Boundary Issues in the Human Services,* and *Ethics Education in Social Work.*

FOR THE READER

The Social Work Ethics Audit: A Risk Management Tool provides practitioners—individual social workers, administrators, supervisors, and educators—with an easy-to-use tool to assess ethics-related policies, practices, and procedures. Based on the latest knowledge concerning professional ethics and risk management, the audit package begins with an overview of key ethical issues and concludes with the practical, concrete steps that social workers can take to address ethical issues in their practice settings. The step-by-step instructions facilitate social workers' comprehensive assessments.

The Social Work Ethics Audit includes three components:

1 A comprehensive *Manual* that provides users with an introduction to the concept of an ethics audit, a succinct overview of the key ethical issues that social workers should assess in their practice settings, and instructions for conducting an ethics audit.
2 The *Audit Instrument*, which contains a comprehensive outline of a wide range of ethics-related policies and procedures that evaluators should examine. The instrument includes a template to help users develop a structured *Action Plan* to address any ethics-related risk areas that require changes in policies or procedures.
3 A *Computer Disk* that provides users with easy access to the Audit Instrument and the template for their Action Plan.

A CAUTIONARY NOTE

The conducting of the ethics audit is only the first step. Practitioners, agencies, and other social work employers who invest the time and energy to audit their ethical compliance should do so only if they have the commitment to correct errors, improve on less than adequate practices, and modify policies or procedures that are lacking (incorrect, out-of-date).

Social workers who conduct an ethics audit should be aware that the audit and its component parts

- are not protected from discovery in a court proceeding.
- are not automatically confidential or subject to the protection of privilege. The documents and files related to the audit should be clearly marked as confidential, for agency use and review only.
- may provide information or data that, unless acted on, could provide evidence in a malpractice claim or ethics complaint.
- may result in an action report that if not implemented may leave the agency or practitioner in a vulnerable, legal, or ethical position.

Questions regarding the potential legal ramifications of the ethics audit or its components should be addressed to an attorney.

The above caution notwithstanding, conducting and following up on the ethics audit can demonstrate a diligent effort on the part of agencies and social workers to identify their strengths and weaknesses and to serve clients well.

MANUAL

Why Conduct an Ethics Audit?

Since the early 1980s, social work's knowledge base related to professional ethics has burgeoned. Social work's literature on the subject has expanded considerably in several key areas: the nature of social work's core values and conflicts between personal and professional values; conflicts among social workers' professional duties and obligations (ethical dilemmas); ethical decision making; ethical misconduct and social worker impairment; and ethics-related malpractice and liability risks (strategies to prevent lawsuits alleging negligence related to, for example, confidentiality, informed consent, social work interventions, boundary issues, and termination of services)(Barker & Branson, 2000; Bernstein & Hartsell, 1998, 2000; Besharov, 1985; Bullis, 1995; Congress, 1998; Gambrill & Pruger, 1997; Houston-Vega, Nuehring, & Daguio, 1997; Loewenberg & Dolgoff, 1996; Reamer, 1990, 1994, 1999).

The Social Work Ethics Audit provides practitioners and agencies with an easy-to-use tool to examine their ethics-related practices, policies, and procedures. *The Social Work Ethics Audit* draws on the latest knowledge in the profession to help social workers enhance quality assurance and promote ethics-related risk management. The primary purpose of *The Social Work Ethics Audit* is to provide practitioners with a practical tool to help them

Identify pertinent ethical issues in their practice settings. What specific ethical risks do social workers face? Are there ethical issues that arise in the work that are unique to the client population, treatment approach, setting, program design, or staffing pattern?

Review and assess the adequacy of their current practices. Has the practice setting addressed compelling ethical issues? How adequate are the current practices, policies, and procedures? What issues need to be addressed?

Design a practical strategy to modify current practices as needed. What steps does the agency or practice need to take to protect clients, prevent disgruntled parties from filing ethics complaints with state licensing boards and professional organizations, and prevent ethics-related lawsuits? Who in the practice or agency should work to address these issues? What resources will they need? What timetable should they follow?

Monitor the implementation of this quality assurance strategy. How can practitioners ensure that the implementation plan has been implemented effectively? What indicators can staff members use to assess the extent to which the audit goals have been met?

The Social Work Ethics Audit can be especially useful to agency administrators who are concerned about ethical and risk-management issues. Administrators in human service agencies—such as family service agencies, community mental health centers, hospitals, nursing homes, schools, and residential treatment programs—need to ensure that staff are knowledgeable about prevailing ethical standards in order to protect clients and prevent ethics complaints and lawsuits. Disgruntled clients and other parties (for example, clients' acquaintances or relatives) may file an ethics complaint with a social worker's state licensing board or with a professional organization (such as the National Association of Social Workers [NASW]). These complaints may lead to formal adjudication and, when there is evidence of ethical violations, sanctions and requirements for corrective action (for example, license suspension or revocation, increased supervision or consultation, continuing education). In addition, clients and other parties may file a lawsuit against a social worker or agency alleging harm that resulted from an ethics violation. These lawsuits typically seek money damages based on allegations that a social worker's ethics-related lapse or misconduct (for example, inappropriate disclosure of confidential information, sexual relationship with a former client, conflict of interest, or financial exploitation of a client) caused significant harm or injury (such as emotional suffering, lost income, or expenses for mental health treatment).

In addition, administrators whose agencies seek accreditation may use *The Social Work Ethics Audit* as a mechanism to review ethical issues and risk-management practices and policies during preparation for the accreditation site visit. The audit provides administrators with a very practical, structured, and organized way to assess key issues. Completion of the audit demonstrates administrators' earnest attempt to review and assess important ethical issues.

Also, individual practitioners can use *The Social Work Ethics Audit* to take a comprehensive and systematic look at the ethical and risk-management aspects of their work. Social workers in agency settings and in independent practice can use this guide to critique their current policies and practices and enhance their risk-management strategies. These steps help to protect clients and prevent ethics complaints and ethics-related lawsuits.

In addition, social work supervisors can use *The Social Work Ethics Audit* to guide their discussions with supervisees about important ethical and risk-management issues. These discussions can prevent ethics-related problems that, if not handled skillfully, could harm clients. Also, supervisors' discussions about topics included in *The Social Work Ethics Audit* can help supervisors to protect themselves in the event that ethics or legal complaints assert that the supervisor's involvement in the case contributed to the alleged unethical conduct or negligent practice (what lawyers call *vicarious liability*).

Finally, social work educators can use this structured guide to educate students and practitioners taking continuing education workshops about key ethical and risk-management issues that they may face in practice.

What Is Contained in an Ethics Audit?

Audits of various types are conducted in many organizations. Ordinarily, an audit entails an "official examination and verification" of records and other organizational practices (*Random House Webster's College Dictionary, 1991*). Both proprietary and nonprofit organizations routinely conduct audits for accounting purposes, quality control and assurance, and utilization review. Audits typically focus on essential aspects of an organization's functioning, such as its bookkeeping procedures; service delivery, personnel, and financial records; and billing practices (Courtemanche, 1989; Russell & Regel, 1996).

This concept and practice can be extended easily and fruitfully to the subject of professional and social work ethics. A social work ethics audit should focus on what is currently considered to be essential or core knowledge in the profession. Social work's literature suggests two key knowledge areas that should form the foundation of the audit: (1) ethics-related risks in practice settings, based on empirical trend data gathered from actual ethics complaints (filed with state licensing boards and professional organizations), lawsuits filed against social workers, and ethics committee and court findings and dispositions; and (2) current agency policies and procedures for handling ethical issues, dilemmas, and decisions (Barker & Branson, 2000; Bernstein & Hartsell, 1998, 2000; Besharov, 1985; Bullis, 1995; Congress, 1998; Gambrill & Pruger, 1997; Houston-Vega, Nuehring, & Daguio, 1997; Joseph, 1989; Loewenberg & Dolgoff, 1996; Reamer, 1990, 1994, 1999; Rhodes, 1986). The structured instrument included in this package, *The Social Work Ethics Audit*, is divided into two main sections focusing on these broad topics. Below is a summary of the major issues and risk areas social workers should address when conducting a thorough ethics audit. (Readers are encouraged to consult in-depth discussions of these ethics-related risks and issues, from sources cited throughout this manual, for further clarification.)

Ethical Risks

A comprehensive ethics audit should assess the extent to which social workers and agencies have practices, procedures, and policies in place to protect clients, identify ethics-related risks, and prevent ethics complaints and ethics-related litigation. This form of risk management is an essential function of an ethics audit. In tort law (a tort involves a private or civil wrong, from the Latin "tortus" or "twisted"), a risk entails a "hazard, danger, or peril, exposure to loss, injury, disadvantage, or destruction. . . . The risk that should be reasonably perceived and avoided defines the common law duty concerning the probability or foreseeability of injury to another" (Gifis, 1991, p. 426).

This section of the audit highlights a number of risks germane to ethical issues encountered in typical social work practice settings. Consistent with longstanding social work principles and values, priority should be given to ethical risks involving imminent and foreseeable harm to clients and others (NASW, 1996). Currently available data and professional standards suggest that there are a number of key risk areas that should be addressed by an ethics audit in an effort to protect clients and prevent ethics complaints and ethics-related lawsuits (Austin, Moline, & Williams, 1990; Barker & Branson, 2000; Bernstein & Hartsell, 1998, 2000; Besharov, 1985; Haas & Malouf, 1995; Houston-Vega, Nuehring, & Daguio, 1997; NASW, 1996; Reamer, 1994: Woody, 1997).

Client rights. The ethics audit should assess whether social workers have developed comprehensive, clearly worded, and comprehensible summaries of clients' rights. In addition, the audit should assess the extent to which practitioners and agencies communicate with clients clearly about each of these rights. Typically such statements address practitioner and agency policy concerning:

- Confidentiality and privacy: Clients have a wide range of confidentiality and privacy rights. Does the practitioner or agency have a clearly worded confidentiality policy that describes clients' rights? Does the document identify exceptions to clients' rights to confidentiality?
- Release of information: Practitioners should have well-established policies and procedures for obtaining client (or guardian) authorization for the release of confidential information. Does the client rights statement describe the procedures that the practitioner or agency uses to obtain client consent prior to releasing confidential information (and any exceptions)?
- Informed consent: Practitioners also should have sound policies and procedures for obtaining client consent to various treatment and service options available to them. Does the client rights statement describe the practitioner's or agency's policy with respect to obtaining client consent in relation to releasing confidential information, treatment alternatives, and activities such as using facsimile communication, videotaping, audiotaping, or permitting observation of services to clients by a third party?
- Access to services: Clients should be informed routinely of their rights to various services offered by their provider. This is especially important in settings where clients are being provided with services involuntarily, for example, prisons, juvenile training facilities, and other programs to which clients are court-ordered. Does the client rights statement describe the extent to which clients are entitled to receive services?
- Access to records: Ordinarily, clients have the right to inspect their records. Social workers who are concerned that clients' access to their records could cause serious misunderstanding or harm to the client should provide assistance in interpreting the records and consultation with the client regarding the records. Only in exceptional circumstances—where there is compelling evidence that a client's access to his or her records would cause serious harm to the client—are social workers permitted to limit clients' access to their records (or portions of their records). Does the client

rights statement summarize the nature of clients' rights to see and obtain copies of information in their records?

- Service plans: Many practitioners seek to include clients in the development of treatment and service plans as a way to empower clients and engage them in the helping process. Does the client rights statement summarize clients' rights to participate in the formulation of service or treatment plans?

- Options for alternative services and referrals: Clients have the right to know whether they can obtain services from other providers. This is consistent with social workers' obligation to respect clients' rights to self-determination and to give informed consent before services are provided to them. Does the client rights statement explain to clients the options that they have to be referred to and receive services from other agencies and providers?

- The right to refuse services: In general, clients have the right to refuse services (there are some exceptions when clients are ordered by a court of law to receive services). Does the client rights statement explain that clients have the right to refuse services and the consequences associated with such refusal?

- Termination of services: Clients should be informed about service providers' policies concerning the termination of services. Does the client rights statement explain the circumstances under which services may or will be terminated, along with relevant criteria and procedures?

- Grievance procedures: In many settings clients have the right to challenge or appeal decisions with which they disagree. These may include decisions about benefits, eligibility for services, or termination of services. Does the client rights statement inform clients of their right to appeal adverse decisions that affect them and of all relevant grievance procedures?

- Evaluation and research: Many agencies involve clients in evaluation or research activities (such as clinical research and program evaluations). Does the client rights statement inform clients of any evaluation or research activities in which they may be involved? Does the document acquaint clients with service providers' policies and procedures designed to protect evaluation and research participants (for example, clients' rights to refuse to participate and confidentiality of research data [see also informed consent above])?

In addition, the audit should assess how regularly and competently social workers inform clients of their rights and assess the procedures used to do so. Do practitioners routinely discuss client rights? Do they discuss these rights thoroughly, systematically, and in a timely fashion? Do practitioners provide clients with an opportunity to ask questions about these rights?

Confidentiality and privacy. An ethics audit should focus considerable attention on a wide range of confidentiality and privacy issues and assess the extent to which they are addressed with clients and in service providers' policies and procedures (Dickson, 1998; Reamer, 1994, 1998). Some confidentiality and privacy issues are unique to professional staff, such as those involving clinical relationships with clients and colleagues. Other confidentiality and privacy issues pertain to nonprofessional staff, such as clerical employees, custodians, and cooks in residential programs; examples include strict guidelines to ensure that nonprofessional staff respect clients' privacy and handle confidential information appropriately. Staff should understand that state confidentiality laws differ; in addition, there may be differences between federal and state confidentiality laws.

Key confidentiality and privacy issues include the following:

- Solicitation of private information from clients: Social workers often have access to sensitive information about intimate aspects of clients' lives, including information about personal relationships, domestic violence, substance abuse, sexual trauma and behavior, criminal activity, and mental illness. Such information is obtained to assess clients' circumstances thoroughly so that social workers can plan and implement appropriate interventions.

  The ethics audit should assess the extent to which social workers respect clients' rights to privacy. Social workers should be conservative in their efforts to obtain private information from clients. That is, they should seek private information from clients only to the extent necessary to carry out their professional functions. Social workers should constantly distinguish between private information that is essential and private information that is gratuitous.

- Disclosure of confidential information to protect clients from self-harm and to protect third parties from harm inflicted by clients: This limitation of clients' rights to confidentiality reflects social workers' increased understanding of two key concepts: professional paternalism and protection of third parties. Professional paternalism means that situations may arise in which social workers have an obligation to protect clients from themselves (Dworkin, 1971; Foster, 1995; Reamer, 1983). The most extreme form of self-injurious behavior is, of course, client suicide, and social workers generally agree that professionals have a duty to interfere with clients' efforts to end their lives. But there are other, more subtle forms of self-harming behavior that pose difficult ethical dilemmas for social workers, for example, when battered women or men decide to resume a relationship with an abusive partner.

  Issues involving the protection of third parties are quite different. Here the justification for social workers' placing limits on clients' rights to self-determination is based on social workers' explicit concern for other people whose well-being is threatened by clients' actions. Unlike cases involving professional paternalism, when social workers are primarily concerned about the client's well-being, circumstances calling for limits on clients' rights to self-determination to protect third parties are those in which social workers must concede that protection and promotion of clients' interests is a secondary consideration.

  The concept of interfering with clients' rights to self-determination to protect third parties is usually associated with the often-cited case of *Tarasoff v. Board of Regents of the University of California* (1976). This case set the precedent for a number of critically important statutes and court decisions that now influence social workers' decisions when clients pose a threat to third parties. Without question, *Tarasoff* changed the way that social workers and other mental health professionals think about the limits of clients' rights to self-determination and confidentiality. Since *Tarasoff*, a number of important duty-to-protect cases have influenced courts and legislatures in situations concerning mental health professionals' duty to protect third parties. Many court decisions and statutes reinforce the court's conclusions in *Tarasoff*, emphasizing practitioners' responsibility to take reasonable steps to protect third parties when, in the professionals' judgment, clients' actions or potential actions pose a serious, foreseeable, and imminent risk to others. Some court decisions, however, challenge, extend, or otherwise modify the conclusions reached in *Tarasoff*.

- Release of confidential information pertaining to alcohol and substance abuse treatment: Strict federal regulations (42 C.F.R. 2-1 ff., "Confidentiality of Alcohol and Drug Abuse Patient Records") limit social workers' disclosure of confidential information. These regulations broadly protect the confidentiality of substance abuse program records—with respect to the identity, diagnosis, prognosis, or treatment of any client—maintained in connection with the performance of any program or activity relating to substance abuse education, prevention, training, treatment, rehabilitation, or research that is conducted, regulated, or directly or indirectly assisted by any federal department or agency. Disclosures are permitted (1) with the written informed consent of the client; (2) to medical personnel in emergencies; (3) for research, evaluation, and audits; and (4) by court order for good cause (Dickson, 1998).
- Disclosure of information about deceased clients: Social workers sometimes receive requests for confidential information about former clients who have died. Surviving family members of a client who has committed suicide may ask for information to help them cope with their loss, or social workers may be subpoenaed in a legal case involving a dispute among family members concerning the former client's will. A reporter or law enforcement official may request information about a deceased client who was the victim of a serious crime, or an Internal Revenue Service agent may seek information about a deceased client's lifestyle.

  Social workers must be diligent in their efforts to protect the confidentiality of deceased clients. They should not disclose confidential information unless they have received proper legal authorization to do so (for example, from the legal representative of the client's estate or by a court order). Disclosure of confidential information without such authorization would constitute a violation of the former client's confidentiality rights.
- Release of information to parents and guardians: Social workers who provide services to minors sometimes must make decisions about the disclosure of confidential information. Typically these situations involve evidence that minor clients are at risk of harming themselves or others, for example, as a result of substance abuse, suicide threats, or high-risk sexual activity.

9

State laws and regulations vary with respect to social workers' obligations in these circumstances. The ethics audit should assess whether service providers' policies and procedures comply with local laws and regulations, specifically concerning the extent to which social workers are (1) obligated to disclose confidential information to parents and guardians, even without the minor client's consent (for example, in the case of a suicide threat), (2) permitted, but not obligated, to disclose confidential information to parents or guardians without the minor client's consent (for example, when a minor client is engaged in high-risk sexual activity), and (3) not permitted to disclose confidential information to parents or guardians without the minor client's consent (for example, when minor clients have the right to seek substance abuse treatment without parental or guardian consent).

- Sharing of confidential information among participants in family, couples, marital, and group counseling: Social workers who provide counseling services to families, couples, or groups face special confidentiality issues. In addition to the usual exceptions to confidentiality found in individual counseling (such as social workers' obligation to disclose information in certain exceptional circumstances involving threats to harm third parties, prevention of suicide, and compliance with mandatory reporting laws and court orders), participants in family, couples, and group counseling also face the possibility that other participants will not respect the right to confidentiality. Social workers should inform clients that they cannot guarantee that other participants will not share information from family, couples, or group counseling with third parties.

  Social workers who provide such clinical services have an obligation to seek agreement among the parties involved in counseling concerning each individual's right to confidentiality and the obligation to respect the confidentiality of information shared by others. Practitioners should consider preparing forms that explain the importance of confidentiality and request each participant's agreement to honor the others' rights to confidentiality.

- Disclosure of confidential information to media representatives, law enforcement officials, protective service agencies, other social service organizations, and collection agencies: Social workers sometimes receive requests for confidential information from third parties who have a vested interest in clients' lives. When this occurs, practitioners need to be vigilant in their efforts to protect clients' confidentiality. For example, if a news reporter discovers that a person who is the subject of a story has been in counseling with a social worker and asks the social worker for specific information about the client, the social worker should respond by informing the reporter that, because of confidentiality requirements, he or she is not permitted to confirm or deny that the individual is or ever has been a client. If a social worker is asked by a reporter to talk about the types of clients that he or she has worked with (for example, perpetrators of childhood sexual abuse), the social worker should speak only in very general terms, without disclosing any details or specific information that might enable the reporter or members of the public to identify individual clients.

Occasionally, clients may want social workers to discuss case-related details with media representatives. In such exceptional circumstances, social workers must be especially careful to obtain truly informed consent. They should discuss with clients in detail the possible risks involved in having the social worker talk openly with members of the media (for example, the risk of experiencing public embarrassment or harassment or of undermining clinical progress) as well as potential benefits (the possible therapeutic value of discussing one's issues openly, the opportunity to educate the public about an important issue).

Social workers should take comparable precautions when they receive requests for confidential information from other sources, such as law enforcement officials, protective service agencies, other social service organizations, and collection agencies. Unless disclosure of such information is legally required (for example, by law or court order), social workers should resist disclosure. In instances where disclosure is required or appropriate, social workers should limit the disclosure as much as possible. For instance, social workers may have a legitimate right to contact a collection agency in an effort to gain payment from clients who have not paid an outstanding balance. In such instances, practitioners should disclose the least amount of information necessary (for example, name, address, telephone number, amount owed) to enable the collection agency to recover the money. Social workers should not disclose clinically relevant details.

- Protection of confidential written and electronic records, information transmitted to other parties through the use of computers, electronic mail, facsimile machines, telephones and telephone answering machines, and other electronic or computer technology: Technological developments have made it possible for social workers to transmit confidential information quickly and efficiently via various electronic media. Along with this convenience and efficiency come considerable risks, primarily involving the inappropriate disclosure of confidential information, that should be examined in the ethics audit. For example, social workers who use facsimile (fax) machines for professional purposes need to be careful to protect clients' privacy and confidentiality. Practitioners who plan to use fax machines to communicate confidential or other sensitive information should first obtain clients' informed consent and inform clients about the potential risks involved (such as security breaches). The confidentiality of faxed communications can be breached in several ways. The receiving fax machine may not be in a secure location (it may be out in the open in a secretary's office, for example); unauthorized parties thus may have access to faxed confidential communications. In addition, the receiving fax machine's telephone number could be misdialed inadvertently, sending the confidential communication to an inappropriate destination.

Although social workers should avoid sending confidential information via fax machine, social workers can take several preventive measures when faxing such information seems necessary (for example, in emergency circumstances). Social workers should notify the recipient by telephone that a fax is being sent and obtain the recipient's agreement to go to the fax machine immediately to await the document's arrival. Ideally, social workers should obtain informed consent from the client authorizing them to convey information via fax. Further, the cover sheet should include a statement alerting recipients to the confidential nature of the communication, along with the sender's telephone number.

Telephones and telephone answering devices also can be problematic. Social workers should avoid discussing confidential information on cellular telephones, for example, because of possible scanner eavesdropping by third parties. Social workers also should be careful not to include confidential information in a message on a telephone answering device when it is possible that the message could be heard by a third party (for example, another member of a client's household or an office mate of a colleague for whom a social worker leaves a message). Social workers routinely should talk with clients about the kind of information that social workers may leave on the clients' telephone answering devices.

In general, social workers should not use the Internet to send confidential information to other parties. It is difficult to ensure that these communications are entirely secure.

- Transfer or disposal of clients' records: Social workers who transfer a case record to another practitioner or agency should take steps to ensure that unauthorized individuals do not have access to confidential information. The ethics audit should examine the extent to which procedures are in place to prevent unauthorized access. For example, delivery services should be selected based on their ability to protect the confidentiality of the information.

The ethics audit also should examine practitioners' procedures for records disposal. Social workers should dispose of records—when appropriate and permitted by relevant regulations, statutes, and standards—in a manner that protects client confidentiality. Records should be shredded or otherwise destroyed so that unauthorized individuals cannot gain access to confidential information.

- Protection of client confidentiality in the event of the social worker's death, disability, or employment termination: Social workers need to anticipate the possibility that at some point they may not be able to continue working with clients because of illness, disability, incapacitation, employment termination, or death. An ethics audit should examine procedures that practitioners put in place to ensure continuity of service and to protect clients' confidential records (for example, making arrangements with colleagues to assume at least initial responsibility for their cases in the event practitioners are unable to continue practicing). Such steps may take the form of oral or written agreements with colleagues or stipulations that appear in a plan that the social worker develops with the assistance of a lawyer (for example, designating a personal representative who will handle the social worker's professional affairs). Many experts recommend that every social worker prepare a will that includes plans for the transfer or disposition of cases in the event of the practitioner's death or incapacitation. The will can provide for an executor or trustee who will maintain records for a certain period of time (30 days, for example), at the end of which the social worker's practice and all records will be sold to a designated colleague (typically for a nominal fee). A major advantage of such arrangements is that they limit unauthorized persons' access to confidential information.

Social workers who expect to retire or move to another community should give clients as much notice as possible and make arrangements to respond to telephone calls or other inquiries from clients (such as arranging for a colleague to respond). Social workers who plan to refer clients to other providers should always give clients several names to avoid the appearance that they are actively "steering" clients. Selected colleagues, supervisors, and administrators should be acquainted with details concerning the handling of the social worker's affairs in the event that he or she terminates practice or becomes unavailable.

- Precautions to prevent social workers' discussion of confidential information in public or semipublic areas such as hallways, waiting rooms, elevators, and restaurants: Ideally, social workers should discuss confidential information only in sound-proofed settings where eavesdropping cannot occur. In reality, social workers sometimes find themselves in circumstances in which confidential information needs to be discussed, or would be convenient to discuss, but where there is a risk that the conversation would be overheard by others (for example, when social workers unexpectedly encounter in a hallway or elevator a colleague with whom they need to consult).

  In these situations, social workers must ensure their clients' privacy to the greatest extent possible. With some effort, social workers can avoid discussing confidential information in agency hallways, waiting rooms, and elevators; in restaurants; at professional conferences; and so on. In other settings, however, it is difficult for social workers to protect the privacy of their discussions of confidential information. For example, some agencies do not provide social workers with individual or private offices. Staff may share an office or have unenclosed or only semipartitioned office space. Although social workers may not have the administrative authority to alter such architecture and office design, they should at least bring their concerns to the attention of appropriate administrators in an effort to have the issue addressed properly.

- Disclosure of confidential information to third-party payers: Social workers routinely receive requests from third-party payers, such as insurance and managed care companies, for information about clients. Such information may include details of a client's mental health symptoms, psychiatric and mental health treatment history, clinical diagnosis, and treatment plan. Ordinarily, third-party payers ask for this information to review requests for mental health and other social services for which the client may be eligible under his or her health insurance coverage.

  Social workers should obtain clients' informed consent before disclosing confidential information to third-party payers. Social workers should provide clients with a clear explanation of the purpose of the consent, risks related to it (for example, office staff who serve the third-party payer would have access to the confidential information), reasonable alternatives (for example, limiting the amount of detail shared with the third-party payer or bypassing the third-party payer entirely by paying for services out of pocket), clients' right to refuse or withdraw consent, and the time frame covered by the consent. Some social workers also include statements in the informed consent or release of information form used for this purpose indicating that the client understands that the social worker cannot be responsible for the protection of the client's confidential information once it is shared with the third-party payer and that the client releases the social worker from any liability connected with a breach of confidentiality by a third-party payer (sometimes called a "hold harmless" clause).

- Disclosure of confidential information to collection agencies: Social workers sometimes have difficulty collecting fees from clients in a timely manner. In extreme circumstances, social workers may contact collection agencies. It is important for social workers to have strict procedures to prevent the inappropriate disclosure of confidential information to collection agencies (such as clinical details). Information shared with these agencies should be limited to the client's name, address, telephone number, and the amount of the debt. Ideally, before services begin, social workers should inform clients of how bad debts will be collected and advise them that bad debts will be turned over to a collection agency or attorney.

- Disclosure of confidential information to consultants: When social workers consult with colleagues about clients, they must be mindful of clients' rights to confidentiality. Although clients may consent to social workers' use of consultants, they may not be comfortable having their social workers share certain confidential information with the consultants. Social workers should obtain clients' informed consent when they need to share confidential information with consultants. In addition, social workers who obtain clients' permission to disclose confidential information to consultants should share the least amount of information necessary to accomplish the purposes of the consultation. This protects clients' confidentiality to the greatest extent possible.

- Disclosure of confidential information for teaching or training purposes: Social work educators and trainers often use case material to illustrate conceptual points, a widely used and respected pedagogical approach in all professions. When presenting case material in classroom or agency settings or at professional workshops or conferences, social workers must be careful to protect clients' confidentiality—identifying information should not be disclosed without clients' informed consent. Social workers who present case illustrations during a lecture, class discussion, workshop, or conference presentation should not mention clients' names and should disguise or alter case-related details to ensure that the audience cannot identify the clients or other individuals involved. One common strategy is to change details concerning clients' gender, age, ethnicity, clinical history, geographical setting, and family circumstances in a way that does not detract from the educational or training goal. Any written case material that a social work educator or trainer distributes should be similarly disguised.

Sometimes social work educators or trainers present videotaped or audiotaped material, especially taped clinical sessions. Such material should not be presented unless clients have provided informed consent to the taping itself and to the presentation of the tape to an audience. With videotapes, it may be possible to protect client confidentiality by taping clients from an angle that limits their visibility or using technological devices to blur distinguishing characteristics or disguise voices, but in some instances (group or family therapy, for example) this may be difficult.

Social workers who seek clients' informed consent to disclose identifying information during teaching or training must use their best judgment as to the clients' ability and competence to make a sound decision. Clients who are asked for their consent may be vulnerable for clinical or other reasons; they may feel pressured to provide their consent to the disclosure when it is not in their best interest to do so. Social workers must be careful not to exploit clients or take advantage of their vulnerability.

Social work educators' responsibilities extend to their students' understanding of confidentiality. That is, social work educators who arrange for or encourage students' presentations of case material must inform students about their obligation to protect client confidentiality. Social work educators should discuss with their students methods that they can use to disguise case material and avoid disclosing identifying information without client consent.

- Protection of confidentiality during legal proceedings: There are many circumstances in which social workers may be asked or ordered to disclose confidential information, especially in the context of civil or criminal court proceedings. Examples include social workers who are subpoenaed to testify in
    - Malpractice cases in which a client has sued another services provider (for example, a physician). The defendant's lawyer may subpoena the client's social worker to have him or her testify about comments that the client made during counseling sessions. The defense lawyer may attempt to produce evidence that the lawsuit merely reflects the client's emotional instability, irrational tendencies, or vindictiveness; the defense also may try to show that the client has a history of mental health problems that preceded the mental health problems that the client has alleged were caused by the defendant in the case. Defense lawyers may use this same strategy in other tort cases in which a social worker's client claims to have been wronged or injured by the actions of another party (for example, as a result of a workplace injury or automobile accident).
    - Divorce proceedings in which a social worker is subpoenaed by one spouse who believes that the social worker's testimony about confidential communications will support his or her claims against the other spouse.
    - Custody disputes in which one parent subpoenas a social worker who has worked with one or both parents, believing that the social worker's testimony will support his or her claim (for example, testimony concerning comments made during a counseling session about one parent's allegedly abusive behavior).

15

- Paternity cases in which, for example, the child's birth mother subpoenas the putative father's social worker, believing that the social worker's testimony concerning the client's comments made during counseling sessions about the couple's sexual relationship may support the birth mother's claim.
- Criminal cases in which a prosecutor or defense attorney subpoenas a social worker to testify about the defendant's comments during counseling sessions.

Social workers may be asked to disclose confidential information during the discovery phase of a legal case or during the court hearing itself. Discovery is a pretrial procedure by which one party obtains information (facts and documents, for example) about the other. During discovery, a social worker may be asked to testify in a deposition under oath, where an attorney poses questions in the same form used in court. Depositions, known as "interrogatories," also may be taken in written form.

Social workers are obligated to protect clients' confidentiality during such legal proceedings to the extent permitted by law. To do so, they need to understand the concepts of privileged communication and subpoenas. The concept of privilege concerns the admissibility of information in court, especially the extent to which courts may compel disclosure of confidential information during legal proceedings (Dickson, 1998; Meyer, Landis, & Hays, 1988; Reamer, 1994). Many states have enacted legislation granting the right of privileged communication to social workers' clients during proceedings in state courts. Further, in the landmark case of *Jaffe v. Redmond* (1996), the U.S. Supreme Court ruled that clinical social workers and their clients have the right to privileged communication in federal courts as well (Alexander, 1997).

Social workers who receive a subpoena to produce records or testify concerning confidential information should attempt to protect clients' confidentiality to the greatest extent possible. If the social worker is subpoenaed in a federal case or by a state court in a state that recognizes the social worker-client privilege, protecting client confidentiality may be easier.

Social workers must understand that it can be a mistake to disclose the information requested in a subpoena. Often social workers can legitimately argue that the requested information should not be disclosed (perhaps because the client has not provided consent or because the disclosure would damage the social worker-client relationship) or can be obtained from some other source. A subpoena itself does not require a social worker to disclose information. Rather, a subpoena is a request for information, and the request may not be an appropriate one (Grossman, 1978; Wilson, 1978).

Social workers who face subpoenas should follow several guidelines (Austin, Moline, & Williams, 1990; Polowy & Gorenberg, 1997; Reamer, 1994, 1998):

- Social workers should not release any information unless they are sure that they have been authorized to do so (for example, in writing or in response to a court order).
- If it is unknown whether the privilege has been waived, social workers

should claim the privilege to protect the client's confidentiality.

- If a social worker employs an assistant or trainee, the claim of privilege should extend to this individual, although the court might rule that unlicensed practitioners are not covered by the privilege.
- At a deposition, when no judge is present, social workers may have their own attorney present or choose to follow the advice and direction of the client's attorney.
- If a social worker's information about a client is embarrassing, damaging, or immaterial, written permission can be obtained to discuss the information with the client's attorney.
- Unless required to produce records or documents only (as with a *subpoena duces tecum*), social workers must appear at the location specified in the subpoena.
- If social workers are asked to appear in court to disclose confidential information and lack a signed release from the client, they should write a letter to the judge stating their wish to comply with the request but noting that the client has not waived the privilege. The court may or may not order disclosure of the information.

Several strategies can be used to protect clients' confidentiality during legal proceedings (Polowy & Gorenberg, 1997). If social workers believe that a subpoena is inappropriate (for example, because it requests information that should be considered privileged under state law), they can arrange for a lawyer (or perhaps the client's lawyer) to file a motion to quash the subpoena, which is an attempt to have the court rule that the request contained in the subpoena is inappropriate. A judge may issue a protective order explicitly limiting the disclosure of specific privileged information during the discovery phase of the case. In addition, social workers, perhaps through a lawyer, may request an *in camera* review (a review in the judge's chambers) of records or documents that they believe should not be disclosed in open court. The judge can then decide whether the information should be revealed in open court and made a matter of public record.

The ethics audit should also assess the adequacy of procedures that social workers use to inform clients of practitioners' and agencies' confidentiality policies. Clients have the right to know how social workers will handle confidential information. Social workers have a responsibility to inform clients about their policies concerning confidentiality, particularly those related to any limitations of clients' rights. Social workers should draw on relevant statutes, regulations, and ethical standards of the profession when developing confidentiality policies.

Ideally, social workers should inform clients of their confidentiality policies early in the social worker-client relationship. In most cases, this can occur during the first meeting with a client. There are some times, however, when this may not be practical (for example, when a new client is in a state of crisis or when the social worker provides services in an emergency). In these situations, social workers should inform clients of their confidentiality policies as soon as possible. Also, occasions arise during the course of practitioners' work with clients when it is appropriate to reacquaint them with confidentiality policies (for example, when a social worker receives an unusual request for confidential information from a third party or is particularly concerned about protecting a third party from harm).

It is most often preferable for social workers to inform clients of their confidentiality policies both orally and in writing. A written summary of a social worker's confidentiality policies can help clients retain the information over time. Clients may be so overwhelmed during their first meeting with a social worker that they find it difficult to remember all the information that the social worker presented. In addition, a written summary signed by the client provides documentation that the social worker conveyed this information to the client.

A social worker's explanation of confidentiality policy should address a number of topics. Depending on the setting, these topics can include
- The importance of confidentiality in the social worker-client relationship (a brief statement of why the social worker treats the subject of confidentiality so seriously)
- Laws, ethical standards, and regulations pertaining to confidentiality (relevant federal, state, and local laws and regulations; ethical standards in social work)
- Specific measures that the social worker will take to protect clients' confidentiality (storing records in a secure location, limiting colleagues' and outside parties' access to records)
- Circumstances in which the social worker would be obligated to disclose confidential information (for example, to comply with mandatory reporting laws or a court order, to protect a third party from harm, or to protect the client from self-injury)
- Procedures that will be used to obtain clients' informed consent for the release of confidential information and any exceptions to this (a summary of the purpose and importance of and the steps involved in informed consent)
- The procedures for sharing information with colleagues for consultation, supervision, and coordination of services (a summary of the roles of consultation, supervision, and coordination of services and why confidential information might be shared)
- Access that third-party payers (insurers) or employee assistance program (EAP) staff will have to clients' records (social workers' policy for sharing information with managed care companies, insurance company representatives, utilization review personnel, and staff of EAPs)
- Disclosure of confidential information by telephone, computer, fax machine, e-mail, and the Internet
- Access to agency facilities and clients by outside parties (for example, people who come to the agency to attend meetings or participate in a tour)
- Audiotaping and videotaping of clients.

The ethics audit should also assess the ways in which the agency or practice setting's physical plant, architecture, and office equipment facilitate or impede protection of confidential information. Do staff have access to locked files for client records? Do staff have access to private office space and meeting rooms for discussion of confidential information? Are confidential electronic records and voicemail messages protected by passwords, codes, and other security measures? Are staff provided with secure wireless telephones for use in the community? Are facsimile machines that receive confidential documents placed in secure locations that limit access?

Informed consent. The ethics audit should closely examine social workers' informed consent documents and procedures (Applebaum, Lidz, & Meisel, 1987; Cowles, 1976; Reamer, 1987a; Rozovsky, 1984; Tomes, 1993; White, 1994). Informed consent is required in a variety of circumstances, including release of confidential information, program admission, service delivery, videotaping, and audiotaping. Although various courts, state legislatures, and agencies have somewhat different interpretations and applications of informed consent standards, there is considerable agreement about the key elements that social workers and agencies should incorporate into consent procedures:

- Coercion and undue influence must not have played a role in the client's decision to consent.
- Clients must be mentally capable of providing consent and able to understand the language and terms used during the consent process.
- Clients must consent to specific procedures or actions, not to broadly worded or blanket consent forms.
- The forms of consent must be valid (although some states require written authorization, most recognize both written and oral consent). All information is written on the form before the client signs it; no information is added after the client has signed the form.
- Clients' written consent is renewed periodically, as needed.
- Clients must have the right to refuse or withdraw consent.
- Clients' decisions must be based on adequate information: details of the nature and purpose of a service or disclosure of information; advantages and disadvantages of an intervention; substantial or possible risks to clients, if any; potential effects on clients' families, jobs, social activities, and other important aspects of their lives; alternatives to the proposed intervention or disclosure; and anticipated costs for clients. All this information must be presented to clients in understandable language and in a manner that encourages them to ask questions. Consent forms also should be dated and include an expiration date. Social workers should be especially sensitive to clients' cultural and ethnic differences related to the meaning of such concepts as "self-determination" and "consent" (Cowles, 1976; Dickson, 1995; President's Commission, 1982; Reamer, 1987b, 1994; Rozovsky, 1984). When necessary, forms should be translated into the clients' primary language and competent interpreters retained.

There are various circumstances in which social workers may not be required to obtain informed consent (Dickson, 1995; Rozovsky, 1984). The most important involve emergencies. In genuine emergencies, professionals may be authorized to act without the client's consent. According to many state statutes and case law, an emergency entails a client's being incapacitated and unable to exercise the mental ability required to make an informed decision. Interference with decision-making ability might be the result of injury or illness, alcohol or drug use, or any other disability. In addition, a need for immediate treatment to preserve life or health must exist. Many statutes also authorize practitioners to treat clients or disclose confidential information without their consent to protect the client or community from harm (Applebaum, Lidz, & Meisel, 1987; Dickson, 1995; President's Commission, 1982; Rozovsky, 1984).

Service delivery. The ethics audit should assess the extent to which social workers provide services and represent themselves as competent only within the boundaries of their education, training, license, certification, consultation received, supervised experience, or other relevant professional experience. Social workers must be forthright and clear in their claims about their areas of competence and expertise to colleagues, potential employers, and the public at large. They must not misrepresent their competence for self-serving purposes (for example, to obtain employment or attract clients).

In addition, the audit should explore whether social workers provide services in substantive areas and use practice approaches, interventions, and techniques that are new to them only after engaging in appropriate study, training, consultation, and supervision from people who are competent in those practice approaches, interventions, and techniques. Appealing innovations that may be relevant to practitioners' work are constantly emerging. Social workers should be aware of and seek education and training about new developments in the field that may be appropriate to incorporate into their work with clients. Sometimes independent education and study may suffice. However, social workers may need to obtain formal training, continuing education, consultation, or supervision to begin work in a new substantive area or use a new intervention technique.

Social workers who obtain training, consultation, or supervision need to ensure that the trainers, consultants, and supervisors themselves are competent. These individuals should have the requisite substantive expertise that the social workers are seeking (specific knowledge about the subject) and the ability to provide effective training, consultation, and supervision.

The ethics audit should focus too on social workers' procedures when they use practice approaches and interventions for which there are no generally recognized standards; in such instances, social workers should obtain appropriate education, training,

- Favors for clients: There are a variety of circumstances when social workers may be tempted, for altruistic reasons, to offer clients favors (for example, giving a stranded client a ride, lending money to a destitute client, giving a vulnerable client one's home telephone number). Although such gestures may be completely innocent and relatively innocuous, social workers should be aware of the ways in which their altruistic instincts may generate boundary issues. In some instances, clients may interpret such gestures as an indication of the social worker's interest in a nonprofessional relationship.

- The delivery of services in clients' homes: Social workers who provide services in clients' homes (for example, when they are on the staff of home health care agencies or programs that provide home-based services for at-risk families) must be particularly alert to potentially problematic boundary issues. Providing services in such non-office, informal, and relatively intimate settings may lead to confusion about the nature of the professional-client relationship. Social workers must be prepared to respond appropriately to family members' invitations to join them for meals, family outings, and other social events.

- Financial conflicts of interest: Introducing financial transactions into the professional-client relationship (for example, when social workers invest in a client's new business venture or borrow money from an affluent client) is likely to distract both practitioners and clients from the social services agenda with which they began their work, compromise clients' interests, and introduce conflicts of interest (where the social worker's judgment and behavior are affected by the financial considerations). Entering into a business relationship with a client is clearly unethical. Also, staff, administrators, and board members should not enter into financial relationships with their agencies or other organizations in a manner that would constitute a conflict of interest (for example, having a personal financial stake in the agency's property, investments, or business transactions). Agencies should have clear policies about staff members' employment in other settings (for example, whether clinical staff at a community mental health center can establish their own part-time private practice) and delivery of services to former clients when staff terminate their employment (for example, when clients choose to transfer their care to their practitioners' new employment setting).

- Delivery of services to two or more people who have a relationship with each other (such as couples or family members): Social workers sometimes provide services to two or more people who have a relationship with each other, often in the context of family, marital, or couples therapy. In these situations, social workers should clarify with all the parties involved which individuals will be considered clients and the nature of the social workers' professional obligations to the various individuals who are receiving services. Social workers who anticipate a conflict of interest among the individuals receiving services or who anticipate having to perform in potentially conflicting roles (for example, when a social worker is asked to testify in a child custody dispute or divorce proceedings involving clients) should clarify their role with the parties involved and take appropriate action to minimize any conflict of interest.

- Barter with clients for goods and services: There are diverse opinions among social workers about the use of barter. Many believe that barter is appropriate in limited circumstances when it can be demonstrated that such arrangements are an accepted practice among professionals in the local community, considered to be essential for the provision of services, negotiated without coercion, and entered into at the client's initiative and with the client's informed consent. Others argue that barter is fraught with risk, particularly when defects in the bartered goods or services lead to conflict in, and hence undermine, the professional-client relationship.

- Management of relationships with clients in small or rural communities: The likelihood of unanticipated boundary issues and dual relationships increases in geographically small communities, especially in rural areas. Social workers in these communities often report how challenging it is to separate their professional and personal lives. Clients may be the proprietors of local businesses that social workers must patronize or may end up being social workers' service providers in other contexts (for example, when a client is the only second-grade teacher in town and the social worker's child is entering that grade). Social workers in these circumstances must be vigilant in their efforts to protect clients, by taking into consideration such factors as the practitioners' own comfort level and confidence in their ability to manage the overlapping relationships; clients' opinions about and perceptions of the boundary issues and their ability to handle them; and the type and severity of the clients' presenting problems. Similar issues can arise in small cultural communities, for example, when a religiously observant social worker employed by a family service agency is actively involved in her religious community and provides services to some members of that community, or a lesbian clinical social worker is actively involved in her local lesbian community and receives requests for services from members of that community.

- Self-disclosure to clients: Social workers' self-disclosure to clients is a complex topic. Social workers generally agree that relatively limited and superficial self-disclosure, handled judiciously, may be appropriate and therapeutically helpful. Social workers also recognize that self-disclosure can harm clients, particularly when the self-disclosure occurs primarily to meet the social worker's own emotional needs. For example, social workers in recovery from substance abuse face unique challenges when they encounter clients at recovery meetings (such as Alcoholics Anonymous or Narcotics Anonymous).

- Collegial relationships with a former client: On occasion, social workers may encounter former clients who have become professional colleagues (for example, former clients who decide to enter the social work field as a result of their personal experiences). In these situations, social workers should discuss with their former clients any problematic boundary issues and ways of dealing with them. In some instances, professional relationships with a former client may not be harmful or risky and may require no special accommodations; in other instances, however, the intensity and complexity of the former professional-client relationship may make a collegial relationship difficult. In these situations, social workers may need to make special arrangements (such as resign from a professional task force on which both parties serve).

■ Hiring former clients: Some social service programs—such as community mental health centers and substance abuse treatment programs—consider hiring former clients or consumers. This practice stems from professionals' belief that, because of their personal experiences, former clients may provide unique and valuable empathy and services to current clients. Hiring former clients is also viewed by many as a way to empower these individuals, promote client growth, and provide current clients with valuable role models.

Social workers need to carefully consider the ethical implications of this practice. In addition to a range of possible benefits, hiring former clients poses several ethics-related risks. Hiring former clients may complicate relationships between practitioners and the former clients who are now agency employees and who must relate to their former service providers as colleagues or employment supervisors. Unique challenges may arise if a former client who is now a staff member needs to re-enter treatment and resume his or her status as client. Also, former clients who were not hired may feel resentful and hurt. Further, hiring former clients may introduce complex issues related to former clients' access to confidential agency records.

For each of these boundary-related risks, social workers need to be familiar with relevant literature, agency policies, regulations, laws, and ethical standards. Further, social workers must develop procedures to enable them to be alert to and avoid real or potential conflicts of interest that interfere with the exercise of professional discretion and impartial judgment (Epstein, 1994; Gutheil & Gabbard, 1993; Herlihy & Corey, 1997; Kagle & Giebelhausen, 1994; Reamer, 2001, in press; Simon, 1999).

Documentation. The ethics audit should assess social workers' documentation styles and procedures. Careful and diligent documentation enhances the quality of services provided to clients. Comprehensive records are necessary to assess clients' circumstances; plan and deliver services appropriately; facilitate supervision; provide proper accountability to clients, other services providers, funding agencies, insurers, utilization review staff, and the courts; evaluate services provided; and ensure continuity in the delivery of future services (Kagle, 1991, 1995; Madden, 1998; Wilson, 1980). Thorough documentation also helps to ensure quality care if a client's primary social worker becomes unavailable because of illness, incapacitation, vacation, or employment termination. In addition, thorough documentation can help protect social workers who are named in ethics complaints or lawsuits (for example, when documentation is needed to demonstrate that a social worker obtained a client's informed consent before releasing confidential information, assessed for suicide risk properly, consulted with knowledgeable experts about a client's clinical issues, or referred a client to other service providers when services were terminated).

In clinical settings, documentation should ordinarily include a number of components (Austin, Moline, & Williams, 1990; Kagle, 1995; Reamer, 1994; Schutz, 1982; Wilson, 1978):

- A complete social history, assessment, and treatment plan that states the client's problems, reason or reasons for requesting services, objectives and relevant timetable, intervention strategy, planned number and duration of contacts, methods for assessment and evaluation of progress, termination plan, and reasons for termination
- Informed consent procedures and signed consent forms for release of information and treatment
- Notes on all contacts made with third parties (such as family members, acquaintances, and other professionals), whether in person or by telephone, including a brief description of the contacts and any important events surrounding them
- Notes on any consultation with other professionals, including the date the client was referred to another professional for service
- A brief description of the social worker's reasoning for all decisions made and interventions provided during the course of services
- Information summarizing any critical incidents (for example, suicide attempts, threats made by the client toward third parties, child abuse, family crises) and the social worker's response
- Any instructions, recommendations, and advice provided to the client, including referral to and suggestions to seek consultation from specialists (including physicians)
- A description of all contacts with clients, including the type of contact (for example, in person or via telephone or in individual, family, couples, or group counseling), and dates and times of the contacts
- Notation of failed or canceled appointments
- Summaries of previous or current psychological, psychiatric, or medical evaluations relevant to the social worker's intervention
- Information about fees, charges, and payment
- Reasons for termination and final assessment
- Copies of all relevant documents, such as signed consent forms, correspondence, fee agreements, and court documents.

It is important for social workers to include only accurate documentation in case records. Records should not be falsified, nor should inaccurate information be included intentionally.

Defamation of character. Related to documentation, the ethics audit should assess the extent to which social workers have training to ensure that their documentation and communication about clients and employees avoid harmful language that rises to the level of defamation of character. In addition to being disrespectful, some forms of pejorative, derogatory, and inaccurate statements can expose social workers to ethical and legal risk. Defamation of character occurs as a result of "the publication of anything injurious to the good name or reputation of another, or which tends to bring him into disrepute" (Gifis, 1991, p.124). It can take two forms: libel and slander. Libel occurs when the publication is in written form (for example, a social worker's progress notes about a client that are read by third parties concerned about the client's circumstances). Slander occurs when the publication is in oral form (for example, when a social worker talks about a client at a staff meeting or provides an oral report about the client's progress to a parole officer or child welfare official). Social workers can be legally liable for defamation of character if they write or say something about a client or colleague that is untrue, if they knew or should have known that the statement was untrue, and if the communication caused some injury to the client or colleague (for example, the client was terminated from a treatment program or the colleague was fired from a job)(Reamer, 1994; Schutz, 1982).

Client records. Social workers should store records following the termination of services to ensure reasonable future access. Records should be maintained for the number of years required by state statutes or relevant contracts. Further, social workers should make special provisions for proper storage and maintenance of records in the event of their disability, incapacitation, termination of practice (because of retirement or disciplinary proceedings, for example), or death. Practitioners should consider working out agreements with colleagues who would be willing to assume responsibility for their records if they are unavailable because of relocation, illness, disability, death, or some other reason.

Supervision. Because of their oversight responsibilities, social work supervisors can be named in ethics complaints and lawsuits alleging ethical breaches or negligence by those under their supervision. These claims often cite the legal principle of *respondeat superior*, which means "let the master respond," and the doctrine of vicarious liability (Reamer, 1994). That is, supervisors may be held partly responsible for actions or inactions in which they were involved only vicariously, or indirectly (Besharov, 1985; Cohen & Mariano, 1982; Hogan, 1979; NASW, 1994; Reamer, 1989). An ethics audit should examine the extent to which social work supervisors

- Provide information necessary for supervisees to obtain clients' informed consent
- Oversee supervisees' efforts to develop and implement thorough treatment and intervention plans
- Identify and respond to supervisees' errors in all phases of client contact, such as the inappropriate disclosure of confidential information
- Know when supervisees' clients need to be reassigned, transferred, or have their treatment terminated
- Know when supervisees should arrange for consultation
- Monitor supervisees' competence and willingness or ability to address any issues concerning incompetence, impairment, and unethical behavior
- Monitor proper boundaries between supervisees and their clients
- Protect third parties
- Detect or stop a negligent treatment plan or treatment carried out longer than necessary

- Determine that a specialist is needed for treatment of a particular client
- Meet regularly with the supervisee
- Review and approve the supervisees' records, decisions, and actions
- Provide adequate coverage in supervisees' absence
- Document supervision provided
- Maintain proper boundaries in relationships with supervisees
- Provide supervisees with timely and informative performance evaluations and feedback
- Listen carefully to supervisees' efforts to raise ethical concerns and issues
- Provide supervisees with sufficient time and appropriate workloads to enable them to meet their professional responsibilities
- Allow sufficient time in their own workloads to provide proper supervision.

To clarify the nature of the supervision that they provide, many supervisors prepare written understandings and agreements to be signed by the supervisor and supervisee. NASW's *Guidelines for Clinical Social Work Supervision* (1994) suggests that such agreements address several key issues:

- Supervisory context: Spell out the purposes and objectives of the supervision, which staff will provide supervision, and any unique supervision methods that will be used (for example, audio or video recordings).
- Learning plan: Identify specific learning goals. Identify any specific bodies of knowledge and skills that will be a priority.
- Format and schedule: Clarify how often supervision will take place, as well as the location, duration, and format (for example, whether individual or group supervision will be provided, whether the supervisor will be available by telephone or e-mail, and whether specific supervision techniques will be used, such as process recordings, role playing, viewing through one-way mirrors, or audio or video recordings).
- Accountability: Spell out the nature of the supervisor's authority within the context of supervision, for example, whether the supervisor will be expected to prepare performance evaluations, provide recommendations for the supervisee's license, or sign case records or claim forms.
- Conflict resolution: Summarize procedures to be used to address conflicts or disagreements between supervisors and supervisees. This may include details concerning possible use of mediation and appeals.
- Compensation: If supervisors will be paid for their services, state who is responsible for payment, the terms of payment, and the mutual obligations and rights of each party.
- Client notification: Include provisions for notifying clients that supervision is taking place, the nature of information that is to be shared, and the supervisor's name and affiliation (or the name and affiliation of someone with administrative authority).
- Duration and termination: Indicate over what period supervision will be provided (for example, beginning and ending dates) and procedures for termination of the supervision.

Staff development and training. The ethics audit should examine training that agencies provide their staff on ethics-related topics. Such training should include a discussion and review of issues related to

- Relevant practice skills
- Professional ethics and liability (especially major risk areas and the phenomenon of ethical decision making)
- Relevant federal, state, and local statutes and regulations
- Assessment tools
- Intervention techniques
- Evaluation methods
- Emergency assistance and suicide prevention
- Supervision of clients in residential programs
- Confidentiality and privileged communication (training should include professional staff, clerical and other nonprofessional staff, and volunteers)
- Informed consent
- Improper treatment and service delivery
- Defamation of character
- Boundary issues in relationships with clients and colleagues (dual and multiple relationships)
- Consultation with and referral to colleagues and specialists
- Fraud and deception
- Termination of services.

Consultation. Social workers often need to or should obtain consultation from colleagues, including social workers and members of other allied professions, who have special expertise. Social workers can be vulnerable to ethics complaints and litigation if they fail to seek consultation when it is warranted or if they consult a colleague with inadequate expertise; this is known as *negligent consultation*. The ethics audit should focus on social workers' procedures to locate and use consultants.

Client referral. Similarly, the ethics audit should assess social workers' policies and procedures concerning client referrals. There are various circumstances in which social workers should refer clients to other professionals. Sometimes clients require specialized assistance that is outside their social workers' areas of expertise. In some circumstances, a social worker and a client may conclude that it would be best for the client to terminate the relationship with the social worker and begin work with another professional. This may occur when a client does not seem to be making satisfactory progress with the social worker or when the client's needs require knowledge and skills outside the social worker's areas of expertise.

Social workers have a responsibility to refer clients to colleagues when social workers do not have the expertise or time to assist clients in need. As part of this process, social workers should refer clients only to colleagues with strong reputations and to practitioners with appropriate credentials. Otherwise, social workers may be accused of *negligent referral*.

Social workers who refer clients to other professionals should follow certain procedures. First, it is important to discuss with clients the reasons for the referral to ensure that both parties agree that the referral makes sense. Social workers should be prepared to respond to a client's possible concerns about the need for or appropriateness of a referral. Second, assuming that choices are available locally, several possible professionals to whom clients might be referred should be carefully considered and discussed with the client. Providing clients with a choice of new providers enhances their options and avoids any suggestion that the social worker is trying to steer the client to particular practitioners. Third, social workers who refer clients to other professionals should disclose, with clients' consent, all pertinent information to the new practitioners. Social workers should discuss with clients which information from the case record is relevant and should be shared with the new service provider. The possible benefits (for example, facilitation of service delivery) and risks (for example, disclosure of private information) associated with such disclosure should be explained to clients. Finally, social workers should follow up with the client once the referral is made to ensure that the client contacted the new provider. Although social workers cannot force clients to contact the new provider, following up with the client demonstrates that the social worker has made an earnest effort to ensure that the client's needs were met.

Fraud. An ethics audit should examine the extent to which social workers have policies and procedures in place to prevent various forms of fraud. Prominent risk areas include fraudulent documentation and billing (Jayaratne, Croxton, & Mattison, 1997; Kirk & Kutchins, 1988). Examples include social workers who deliberately submit embellished insurance claim forms or vouchers for travel expenses, forge supervisors' signatures on official forms, arrange for psychiatrists to "sign off" on insurance claim forms as if they were directly involved in a client's treatment, falsify statistics on use of services, or complete informed consent forms after clients have signed them. Practice settings should have procedures in place to ensure that staff do not, for instance, falsify employment applications, falsify case records (for example, recording that home visits occurred when they did not or that client consent was obtained when it was not), exaggerate clinical diagnoses to obtain third-party payment, or bill third-party payers for services that were not provided.

Termination of services and client abandonment. Termination is a critically important risk area, particularly in light of current managed care policies and procedures (Reamer, 1997; Schamess & Lightburn, 1998; Strom-Gottfried, 1998). Social workers expose themselves to risk when they terminate services improperly (for example, when a social worker leaves an agency relatively suddenly without adequately referring a client in need to another practitioner or terminates services to a vulnerable client who has not paid an outstanding balance). Social workers may also be at risk if they do not terminate services properly when a client is noncompliant, are not reasonably available to clients, or do not properly instruct them about how to handle emergencies that may arise.

In general, these problems pertain to what lawyers call *abandonment*. Abandonment is a legal concept that refers to instances when a professional is not available to a client when needed. Once social workers begin to provide services to a client, they incur an ethical and legal responsibility to continue that service or to properly refer a client to another competent service provider. Hence, the ethics audit should assess the adequacy of social workers' termination criteria and procedures. Social workers should take a number of steps to avoid abandoning clients (Austin, Moline, & Williams, 1990; Reamer, 1994; Schutz, 1982):

- Consult with colleagues and supervisors about a decision to terminate services. In some cases addressing relevant issues can prevent termination. For example, social workers may be able to address a client's reason for not paying an overdue balance and develop a workable payment plan. Social workers whose clients are not making reasonable progress may be able to modify their intervention to enhance the clients' progress.
- Give as much advance warning as possible to clients who will be terminated.
- Provide clients with the names, addresses, and telephone numbers of at least three appropriate referrals when it is necessary to terminate services.
- When clients announce their decision to terminate prematurely, explain to them the risks involved and offer suggestions for alternative services. Include this information in a follow-up letter.
- In cases involving discharge of a client from a residential facility, be sure that a comprehensive discharge plan has been formulated and significant others have been notified of the client's discharge (the client should be informed of this). In cases involving court-ordered clients, seek legal consultation and court approval before terminating care.
- Follow up with a client who has been terminated. If he or she does not go to the referral, write a letter to the client about the risks involved should he or she not follow through with the referral.
- Provide clients with clear instructions to follow and telephone numbers to use in case of emergency. Include a copy of these instructions in their case records. Ask clients to sign this copy, indicating that they received the instructions and the instructions were explained to them.
- When away from the office for an extended time, call in regularly for messages. Social workers who are away from the office should leave an emergency telephone number with a secretary, an answering service, or an answering device. Social workers who anticipate that certain clients may need assistance during their absence should refer those clients to a colleague with appropriate expertise.
- Social workers who are leaving an employment setting (for example, to start a new job) should inform clients of appropriate options for the continuation of services

31

(such as transferring to another service provider or continuing with the social worker in his or her new employment setting) and of the benefits and risks of the options.

- Carefully document in the case record all decisions and actions related to termination of services.

Practitioner impairment. All professions need to be concerned about the possibility of impaired practitioners, or colleagues whose functioning falls below acceptable standards (Barker & Branson, 2000; Berliner, 1989; Besharov, 1985; Bullis, 1995). A significant percentage of ethics complaints and lawsuits are filed against social workers who meet the definition of impaired professional (Reamer, 1992, 1994). Reflecting growing recognition of this phenomenon, several standards specific to this subject were added to the 1993 NASW *Code of Ethics* for the first time and retained in the 1996 code.

Impairment may involve failure to provide competent care or violation of social work's ethical standards. It may also take such forms as providing flawed or inferior services, sexual involvement with a client, or failure to carry out professional duties as a result of substance abuse or mental illness (Lamb et al., 1987). Such impairment may be the result of a wide range of factors, such as employment stress, illness or death of family members, marital or relationship problems, financial difficulties, midlife crises, personal physical or mental health problems, legal problems, and substance abuse (Bissell & Haberman, 1984; Guy, Poelstra, & Stark, 1989; Thoreson, Miller, & Krauskopf, 1989).

In light of the importance of the subject of impaired practitioners, the ethics audit should examine the extent to which social workers understand the nature of professional impairment and its possible causes, are alert to warning signs, and have procedures in place to prevent, identify, and respond appropriately to impairment. Ideally, social workers' efforts to address impairment among colleagues would include several components (Fausel, 1988; Schoener & Gonsiorek, 1988; Sonnenstuhl, 1989; VandenBos & Duthie, 1986):

- Social workers need to be able to recognize and acknowledge impairment when it exists.
- Social workers should have some understanding of the causes of impairment.
- When feasible, social workers should be willing to approach colleagues who appear to be impaired, discuss their concerns, and suggest possible remedies or corrective action (what Sonnenstuhl, 1989, called "constructive confrontation").
- If efforts to work with an impaired colleague are not successful, social workers should take action through appropriate channels established by employers, agencies, NASW, licensing and regulatory bodies, and other professional organizations (such as professional associations that certify social workers to use particular treatment approaches or to work with particular groups of clients).

Further, social workers who become aware of their own impairment have an obligation to take steps to remedy the situation. Options include seeking appropriate consultation and professional help, making adjustments in workload, and, when necessary, terminating practice.

Evaluation and research. Many human service agencies conduct research and evaluation to enhance practice effectiveness and contribute knowledge to the social work profession and the broader society. These efforts use a variety of research methods—such as single-case designs, control-group designs, surveys, interviews, questionnaires, observation, and secondary data analysis—and focus on clinical dynamics and outcomes, program effectiveness, policy implementation, and administrative initiatives.

The ethics audit should assess policies and procedures designed to evaluate services and programs, contribute new knowledge, and protect participants in these diverse research and evaluation activities (Grinnell, 1997; Reamer, 1998; Rubin & Babbie, 1997). The audit should focus specifically on policies and procedures that encourage practitioners to

- Conduct research and evaluate programs, policies, and services
- Keep current with emerging knowledge relevant to social work and use evaluation and research evidence in their professional practice
- Follow guidelines developed for the protection of evaluation and research participants (including consultation of appropriate institutional review boards)
- Obtain voluntary and written informed consent from evaluation and research participants, when appropriate
- Inform participants of their right to withdraw from evaluation and research at any time without penalty
- Take appropriate steps to ensure that participants in evaluation and research have access to appropriate supportive services
- Protect evaluation and research participants from unwarranted physical or mental distress, harm, danger, or deprivation
- Discuss collected information only for professional purposes and only with people professionally concerned with this information
- Ensure the anonymity or confidentiality of participants and of the data obtained from them, to the extent permitted by law and regulation
- Protect research and evaluation participants' confidentiality by omitting identifying information unless proper consent has been obtained authorizing disclosure
- Report evaluation and research findings accurately
- Avoid conflicts of interest and dual relationships with evaluation and research participants

Ethical Decision Making

A significant portion of ethics complaints and ethics-related lawsuits arise out of difficult ethical dilemmas encountered by social workers. That is, complainants often allege that social workers mishandled ethical dilemmas or exercised poor judgment.

Since the early 1980s, most professions, including social work, have developed protocols to help practitioners make difficult ethical decisions when they encounter ethical dilemmas (Loewenberg & Dolgoff, 1996; Reamer, 1999). Ethical dilemmas occur when social workers encounter conflicting professional duties and obligations. Such conflicts may occur in clinical social work, administration, community organizing and advocacy, research, and policy formation. In philosophical language, ethical dilemmas entail conflicts among *prima facie duties* (Ross, 1930), that is, conflicts among duties that social workers are ordinarily obligated to fulfill.

The ethics audit should assess social workers' familiarity with the variety of ethical dilemmas germane to their practice setting and the procedures that they use to make ethical decisions. Clinical social workers should be familiar with ethical dilemmas that occur among such potentially conflicting duties as protecting client confidentiality, respecting clients' rights to self-determination, respecting clients' social and cultural norms, protecting clients and third parties from harm, being truthful, and maintaining clear professional boundaries (Dean & Rhodes, 1992; Loewenberg & Dolgoff, 1996; Reamer, 1998, 1999). For example, ordinarily social workers are inclined to respect clients' rights to self-determination *and* to protect clients from harm. On occasion, however, clients exercise their rights to self-determination in ways that are likely to cause harm to themselves (for example, when a homeless client decides to sleep outdoors in below-freezing weather or when a battered woman informs her social worker that she plans to return home yet again to her abusive partner, consistent with her ethnic community's norms).

In contrast, social work administrators should be familiar with ethical dilemmas involving the allocation of scarce or limited resources (what moral philosophers refer to as problems of distributive justice), being truthful, and adhering to relevant regulations, policies, and laws (Kurzman, 1983; Levy, 1982). For example, a social work administrator may find himself caught between his obligation to be truthful and his duty to withhold potentially damaging information from newspaper reporters who are investigating alleged fraud at the agency. The director of an affordable housing program for low-income people may struggle to determine the most ethical approach to allocating a relatively small number of subsidized housing units among a large number of applicants (for instance, whether to allocate this limited resource based on need, affirmative action criteria, a lottery, or a first come-first served basis). A community organizer might find herself caught between her duty to support neighborhood residents' rights to self-determination and her obligation to challenge residents' racist efforts to drive out low-income neighbors of color under the guise of urban renewal. A social work supervisor might face a difficult choice between protecting an agency's reputation (and future funding) and exposing ethical misconduct on the part of the agency's executive director. In these instances, social workers must reconcile conflicting duties and obligations in a manner that is consistent with the profession's values and ethical standards.

The ethics audit should assess social workers' familiarity with and use of recently developed decision-making protocols designed to address such ethical dilemmas, including their specific components. Most of these protocols include an outline of steps that practitioners can follow to help them approach ethical dilemmas systematically, drawing especially on ethical theory; relevant professional literature; statutes, regulations, codes of ethics and policies; and consultation. For example, one decision-making protocol entails seven steps (Reamer, 1999; also see Congress, 1998; Joseph, 1985, and Loewenberg & Dolgoff, 1996):

I   Identify the ethical issues, including the social work values and duties that conflict.

II   Identify the individuals, groups, and organizations that are likely to be affected by the ethical decision.

III   Tentatively identify all possible courses of action and the participants involved in each, along with possible benefits and risks for each.

IV   Thoroughly examine the reasons in favor of and opposed to each possible course of action, considering relevant (a) ethical theories, principles, and guidelines; (b) codes of ethics and legal principles; (c) social work practice theory and principles; (d) personal values (including religious, cultural, and ethnic values and political ideology).

V   Consult with colleagues and appropriate experts (such as agency staff, supervisors, agency administrators, attorneys, ethics scholars, and ethics committees).

VI   Make the decision and document the decision-making process.

VII   Monitor, evaluate, and document the decision.

Some of the elements of this decision-making protocol require technical knowledge and skill. With regard to step IV, for example, the ethics audit should assess the extent to which social workers are familiar with widely taught ethical theories, principles, and guidelines. Social work students, and students in other professions, are now routinely acquainted with standard ethical theory that, until the early 1980s, was addressed primarily in traditional moral philosophy and ethics courses rather than in professional education (Callahan & Bok, 1980). In the early 1980s, however, the various professions began to recognize the relevance of ethical theory to professionals' attempts to grapple with difficult ethical judgments. Consequently, social workers are now taught about classic theories of *normative ethics*, including what philosophers refer to as *deontological, consequentialist, utilitarian,* and *virtue* theory. These diverse philosophical perspectives are commonly used to analyze ethical dilemmas from different conceptual angles. (For in-depth discussions of these different philosophical perspectives, see Frankena, 1973; Hancock, 1974; Rachels, 1993; Reamer, 1993, 1999.)

Use of relevant codes of ethics, another component of step IV, also requires specialized knowledge, especially since the ratification of the 1996 NASW *Code of Ethics*. The 1996 code—only the third formal code in NASW's history—constitutes a sea-change in the profession's ethical standards (Reamer, 1998). The first NASW code, ratified in 1960, was only one page and included fourteen broadly worded "proclamations" concerning, for example, every social worker's duty to give precedence to professional responsibility over personal interests; to respect the privacy of clients; to give appropriate professional service in public emergencies; and to contribute knowledge, skills, and support to human service programs.

In contrast, the 1996 NASW *Code of Ethics* contains an enormous range of much more specific content relevant to contemporary practice. In addition to a newly constructed mission statement for the profession and a relatively brief description of core social work values and broad ethical principles, the code includes 155 specific ethical standards to guide social workers' conduct and provide a basis for adjudication of ethics complaints filed against NASW members. (The code, or portions of it, is also used by many state licensing boards charged with reviewing complaints filed against licensed social workers and by courts of law that oversee litigation involving alleged social worker negligence or misconduct.) The social work ethics audit should pay particular attention to the code's standards that address concrete ethics-related risks, for example, confidentiality (1.07), informed consent (1.03), competence (1.04, 2.10), client records (1.08, 3.04), conflicts of interest (1.06, 1.09, 1.10), fraud (4.04), interruption and termination of services (1.15, 1.16), supervision and consultation (2.05, 3.01), referral (2.06), practitioner impairment (2.09, 4.05), evaluation and research (5.02). In light of these available resources, the social work ethics audit should also assess the extent to which social workers avail themselves of consultation when they encounter ethical dilemmas, consult ethics committees, address codes of ethics, and conduct an ethics audit.

How Do I Conduct an Ethics Audit?

Steps in an Ethics Audit

Conducting the actual ethics audit involves several key steps.

1 In agency settings, a staff member should assume the role of chair of the ethics audit committee. Members should be appointed to the committee based on their demonstrated interest in the agency's ethics-related policies and practices. Ideally, the chair would have obtained formal education or training related to professional ethics. Individual practitioners may want to consult with knowledgeable colleagues or a peer supervision group.

2 Using the topical outline contained in the ethics audit as a guide, the committee should identify specific ethics-related issues on which to focus. In some settings the committee may decide to conduct a comprehensive ethics audit, one that addresses all of the topics. In other agencies, the committee may focus on specific ethical issues that are especially important in those settings.

3 The ethics audit committee should decide what kind of data it will need to conduct the audit. Data may be gathered from documents and from interviews conducted with agency staff that address specific issues contained in the audit. For example, staff may examine the agency's clients' rights and informed consent forms. In addition, staff may interview or administer questionnaires to "key informants" in the agency about such matters as the extent and content of ethics-related training that they have received or provided, specific ethical issues that need attention, and ways to address compelling ethical issues. Staff may want to consult a lawyer about legal issues (for example, the implications of state confidentiality laws or key court rulings) and agency documents (for example, the appropriateness of agency informed consent and release-of-information forms). Also, staff should review all relevant regulations and laws (federal, state, and local) and ethics codes in relation to confidentiality, privileged communication, informed consent, client records, termination of services, supervision, licensing, personnel issues, and professional misconduct.

4 Once the necessary data are gathered and reviewed, the ethics audit committee should assess the risk level associated with each topic. The assessment for each topic is divided into two sections: policies and procedures. The ethics audit requires separate assessment of the adequacy of various ethics-related policies and procedures. Policies may be codified in formal agency documents or memoranda (for example, official policy concerning confidentiality, informed consent, dual relationships, and termination of services). Procedures entail social workers' actual handling of ethical issues in their relationships with clients and colleagues (for example, concrete steps staff take to address ethical issues involving confidentiality or collegial impairment, routine explanations provided to clients concerning agency policies about informed consent and confidentiality, ethics consultation obtained, informed consent forms completed, documentation placed in case records in ethically complex cases,

supervision and training provided on ethics-related topics).

Each topic addressed in the audit should be assigned one of four risk categories: (1) no risk—current practices are acceptable and do not require modification; (2) minimal risk—current practices are reasonably adequate; minor modifications would be useful; (3) moderate risk—current practices are problematic; modifications are necessary to minimize risk; and (4) high risk—current practices are seriously flawed; significant modifications are necessary to minimize risk. Evaluators should insert the appropriate point value in the space next to each topic in the lists provided on the audit instrument.

5 Once an ethics audit has been completed, social workers need to take assertive steps to make constructive use of its findings. Social workers should develop an "Action Plan" for each risk area that warrants attention. Areas that fall into the "high risk" category should receive immediate attention. These are areas that jeopardize clients and expose social workers and their agencies to serious risk of ethics complaints and litigation. Areas that fall into the "moderate risk" and "minimum risk" categories should receive attention as soon as possible.

In agency settings, administrators are often the most appropriate individuals to oversee efforts to address problem areas identified in an ethics audit. In some cases, administrators may want to appoint a special task force or committee to address the issues, apart from the ethics audit committee. An increasing number of agencies have established "institutional ethics committees" (IECs) that can assume this responsibility (Conrad, 1989; Reamer, 1987b). IECs, which were first introduced in 1976 as a result of a New Jersey Supreme Court ruling in the Karen Ann Quinlan case, may be a very useful mechanism to address problem areas identified by an ethics audit, for example, antiquated informed consent forms, incomplete confidentiality policies, and inadequate procedures for the termination of services.

6 Establish priorities among the areas of concern, based on the degree of risk involved and available resources.

7 Spell out specific measures that need to be taken to address the identified problem areas. Examples include reviewing all current informed consent forms and creating updated versions; writing new, comprehensive confidentiality policies; creating a clients' rights statement; inaugurating training of staff responsible for supervision; strengthening staff training on documentation and on boundary issues; and preparing detailed procedures for staff to follow when terminating services to clients. Identify all of the resources needed to address the risk area, such as agency personnel, publications, staff development time, appointment of a committee or task force, legal consultants, and ethics consultants.

8 Identify which staff will be responsible for the various tasks and establish a timetable for completion of each. Have a lawyer review and approve policies and procedures to ensure compliance with relevant laws, regulations, and court opinions.

9 Identify a mechanism to follow up on each task to ensure its completion and monitor its implementation.

10 Document the complete process involved in conducting the ethics audit. This documentation may be helpful in the event of a lawsuit alleging ethics-related negligence (in that it provides evidence of the agency's or practitioner's conscientious effort to address specific ethical issues). It may also be useful when agencies undergoing accreditation must demonstrate how they have addressed a wide variety of ethical issues.

Case Illustration

The executive director of a family service agency in a major metropolitan area attended a workshop on social work ethics. At the workshop the social worker was introduced to the concept of an ethics audit and decided to conduct one in her agency. During the workshop the administrator realized that at least several of her agency's practices were not in compliance with current ethical standards and, as a result, posed a risk to the agency's clients and the agency itself. The administrator was especially concerned because the agency was scheduled to be reviewed for re-accreditation.

The administrator delegated oversight of the ethics audit to the agency's associate director. The associate director convened a meeting of the agency's division and program managers, reviewed the concept of an ethics audit, and brainstormed with staff strategies that they could use to gather the necessary information. By the end of the first meeting the staff agreed that the information would need to be acquired from several sources, including existing agency documents (for example, clients' rights statements, informed consent forms, confidentiality statements, personnel procedures), self-administered questionnaires completed by staff concerning various agency practices (for example, supervision protocols, referral procedures, procedures commonly used to terminate services), and in-person interviews with management staff concerning highly sensitive subjects (for example, perceptions concerning impaired colleagues, proposals to respond to impairment). The staff also agreed that they could enhance the quality and credibility of the audit by including two external consultants on their task force (the outside consultants included the executive director of a local agency who once chaired the NASW state chapter's Committee on Inquiry and a local social work educator who was knowledgeable about social work ethics).

Once the data were gathered and collated, copies of all the relevant documents and survey and interview results were distributed to the committee members. Time was scheduled for the committee to review and discuss the results and, as a group, review each item addressed in the audit and assign a rating (that is, no risk, minimal risk, moderate risk, or high risk). When the task force was unable to reach consensus about a topic's risk category, the group members' individual ratings were averaged, with the topic placed in the risk category corresponding most closely to the group mean.

Results of the ethics audit indicated that the family service agency faced several "high risk" issues. These included a need to update the agency's confidentiality policy, develop procedures to protect electronically stored client records, develop a clients' rights statement, revise informed consent forms and procedures to comply with current legal

39

standards, and develop a policy on staff's relationships (especially sexual and social) with former clients. A number of other issues fell into the "moderate risk" and "minimal risk" categories, such as the need for a written protocol to guide staff supervision, guidelines for documentation and case recording, and formation of a committee to develop an in-service training curriculum related to the NASW *Code of Ethics* and strategies for ethical decision making.

Once the topics were placed in rank-ordered risk categories, the task force discussed steps that they could take to address the issues considered high risk; the task force also discussed their timetable and the resources needed to address the issues. In addition, the task force discussed whether to wait until the "high risk" issues were addressed before proceeding with the "moderate risk" and "minimal risk" issues. The task force agreed that two of the "moderate risk" and "minimal risk" issues could be addressed simultaneously (formation of an in-service training committee and development of a written protocol to guide staff supervision), while the others should wait until the "high risk" issues were addressed.

Within a six-month period, all of the "high risk" issues but one were addressed to the task force's satisfaction. The exception involved the development of guidelines concerning staff members' relationships with former clients; staff disagreed about the nature of appropriate limitations on these relationships. They agreed to take some time to survey other family service agencies' policies, review relevant literature on the subject of professional boundaries, and consult with nationally known experts on social work ethics in an effort to achieve more insight and consensus on the issue.

After the staff embarked on their efforts to address the various "high risk" categories, they turned to the "moderate" and "minimal" risk issues. They focused on strengthening their in-service training curriculum related to the NASW Code of Ethics and ethical decision making. Senior staff organized and implemented a four-session training schedule to increase employees' knowledge of ethical standards in social work and their ability to make sound decisions when faced with ethical dilemmas. A staff member responsible for the training prepared three case studies drawn from published literature and the agency's own experiences. After distributing the case studies and facilitating initial discussion of the issues, the trainer provided staff with an overview of an ethical decision-making model and reviewed pertinent ethical standards (drawing especially on the NASW Code of Ethics and the state's social work licensing regulations). The trainer then divided the staff into small groups to apply the decision-making framework to the case studies. Later, the staff reconvened as a large group and representatives from each of the small groups summarized their group's discussion. Because two of the cases involved legal issues and potential malpractice risks, the trainer arranged for a local attorney who often advises the agency on legal matters to participate in the discussion. At the conclusion of the four sessions, the trainer summarized what the staff had learned about prevailing ethical standards in the profession and the process that they had learned to use to make difficult ethical decisions.

Conclusion

The remarkable maturation of ethical standards in a number of pertinent areas—such as confidentiality and privacy, service delivery, professional boundaries, informed consent, defamation of character, fraud, consultation and referral, practitioner impairment, and termination of services—has accelerated the need for social workers to examine more closely the ethical dimensions of their practice.

The social work ethics audit is a process designed to help social workers assess ethical issues systematically and comprehensively. The content of the audit reflects the most current knowledge available related to social work ethics—knowledge that has advanced dramatically in recent years. The process of an ethics audit is designed to help social workers identify relevant ethical issues in their practice settings, assess risk levels, rank order each issue, and develop a strategy to address each risk area.

In addition to embracing the concept of an ethics audit, social workers must think critically about who should conduct such assessments. Clearly, self-auditing—by individual practitioners and social service agencies—can be useful. Self-auditing can also be self-serving and shortsighted, however, particularly when there are incentives to overlook ethics-related problems. Social work ethics audits may be especially valuable when they are conducted by independent parties outside of one's practice or agency, much like the agency accreditation process.

Also, despite the structure, formality, and apparent objectivity of the social work ethics audit process, social workers must recognize that any assessment of this nature necessarily involves considerable subjective judgment. Certainly, it is useful to structure and routinize an ethics audit; however, social workers must recognize that the auditor's own values, ethical instincts, ideological biases, formal authority, and political status will influence the outcome. Realistically, organizational dynamics and politics may affect both the audit process and results.

The concept of an ethics audit is consistent with social work's enduring efforts to protect clients and prevent ethics-related breaches. Such systematic attempts to highlight, address, and monitor the ethical dimensions of social work practice will, in the final analysis, strengthen the profession's integrity.

AUDIT INSTRUMENT

Instructions

The Social Work Ethics Audit includes an assessment of practitioners' and agencies' practices in a number of key areas. The structured outline includes a wide range of ethics-related policies and procedures that evaluators should examine. Staff responsible for the ethics audit should proceed as follows:

Gather the information necessary to assess the level of risk associated with each topic (for example, agency documents, laws, regulations, NASW *Code of Ethics*, data gathered from interviews with agency staff).

Review all available information.

Assign one of four risk scores to each topic below:
- **1 point**   **no risk:** *current practices are acceptable and do not require modification*
- **2 points**   **minimal risk:** *current practices are reasonably adequate; minor modifications would be useful*
- **3 points**   **moderate risk:** *current practices are problematic; modifications are necessary to minimize risk*
- **4 points**   **high risk:** *current practices are seriously flawed; significant modifications are necessary to minimize risk*

Topics that are not applicable receive a score of 0.

Identify all topics scored as "high risk."

Prepare an Action Plan for each "high risk" topic using the template provided at the end of this instrument. Address (1) the steps required to reduce risk, (2) the resources required, (3) the personnel who will oversee the Action Plan, (4) the timetable for completion of the Action Plan, (5) indicators of progress toward minimizing risk, and (6) plans to monitor implementation of the Action Plan.

Repeat this process for each topic identified as "moderate" and "minimal" risk.

Part I: Ethical Risks

Client rights: The agency has appropriate policies and procedures concerning clients' rights.

POLICIES

1 point   **no risk:** *comprehensive policies exist concerning clients' rights consistent with relevant laws, regulations, and ethical standards*

2 points   **minimal risk:** *policies concerning clients' rights exist, but require minor revision*

3 points   **moderate risk:** *policies concerning clients' rights exist, but require significant revision; policies concerning some clients' rights need to be created*

4 points   **high risk:** *existing policies are inadequate or are seriously flawed; policies need to be created to address a significant number of clients' rights*

_____ Confidentiality and privacy

_____ Informed consent and release of information

_____ Options for services and referrals

_____ Access to records

_____ Right to participate in formulation of service plans

_____ Right to refuse services

_____ Termination of services

_____ Grievance procedures

_____ Protection of evaluation and research participants

PROCEDURES

1 point   **no risk:** *social workers routinely provide clients with clear information about their rights in each of the following areas*

2 points   **minimal risk:** *social workers usually provide clients with clear information about their rights in each of the following areas, but there are exceptions*

3 points   **moderate risk:** *social workers are very inconsistent in their efforts to inform clients about their rights*

4 points   **high risk:** *social workers rarely or never provide clients with information about their rights*

_____ Confidentiality and privacy

_____ Informed consent and release of information

_____ Options for services and referrals

_____ Access to records

_____ Right to participate in formulation of service plans

_____ Right to refuse services

_____ Termination of services

_____ Grievance procedures

_____ Protection of evaluation and research participants

Confidentiality and privacy: The agency has appropriate policies and procedures concerning confidentiality and privacy.

POLICIES

1 point **no risk:** *clear, comprehensive policies exist concerning client confidentiality and privacy in each of the following areas, consistent with relevant laws, regulations, and ethical standards*

2 points **minimal risk:** *policies concerning client confidentiality and privacy exist, but require minor revision*

3 points **moderate risk:** *policies concerning client confidentiality and privacy exist, but require significant revision; policies concerning some confidentiality and privacy issues need to be created*

4 points **high risk:** *existing policies are inadequate or are seriously flawed; policies need to be created to address a significant number of confidentiality and privacy issues*

_____ Laws, ethical standards, and regulations pertaining to confidentiality (relevant federal, state, and local laws and regulations; ethical standards in social work)

_____ Specific measures that the social worker will take to protect clients' confidentiality (storing records in a secure location, limiting colleagues' and outside parties' access to records)

_____ Procedures that will be used to obtain clients' informed consent for the release of confidential information and any exceptions to this

_____ Procedures for sharing information with colleagues for consultation, supervision, and coordination of services and why confidential information might be shared

_____ Solicitation of private information from clients

_____ Disclosure of confidential information to protect clients from self-harm and to protect third parties from harm

_____ Release of confidential information pertaining to alcohol and substance abuse treatment and services

_____ Disclosure of confidential information about deceased clients

_____ Release of confidential information to minor clients' parents or guardians

_____ Sharing of confidential information among parties in family, couples, marital, and group counseling

_____ Disclosure of confidential information to media representatives, law enforcement officials, protective services agencies, other social services agencies, and collection agencies

_____ Protection of confidential written and electronic records, information transmitted to other parties through the use of computers, electronic mail, facsimile machines, telephones and telephone answering machines, and other electronic or computer technology

_____ Transfer and disposal of clients' records

_____ Protection of client confidentiality in the event of the social worker's death, disability, or employment termination

_____ Precautions to prevent discussion of confidential information in public or semipublic areas

_____ Disclosure of confidential information to third-party payers

_____ Disclosure of confidential information to consultants

_____ Disclosure of confidential information when discussing clients for teaching or training purposes

_____ Protection of client confidentiality during legal proceedings

_____ Protection of client confidentiality during research and evaluation

_____ Providing staff with appropriate office space and meeting areas to ensure confidentiality and privacy

_____ Providing staff with appropriate office equipment and technology to ensure confidentiality and privacy (for example, secure file cabinets, wireless telephones, computer files, and facsimile machines)

PROCEDURES

1 point **no risk:** *practitioners routinely follow procedures related to confidentiality and privacy in each of the following areas*

2 points **minimal risk:** *practitioners usually follow procedures related to confidentiality and privacy in each of the following areas, but there are exceptions*

3 points **moderate risk:** *practitioners are very inconsistent in their use of procedures related to confidentiality and privacy*

4 points **high risk:** *practitioners rarely or never follow procedures related to confidentiality and privacy*

_____ Laws, ethical standards, and regulations pertaining to confidentiality (relevant federal, state, and local laws and regulations; ethical standards in social work)

_____ Specific measures that the social worker will take to protect clients' confidentiality (storing records in a secure location, limiting colleagues' and outside parties' access to records)

_____ Procedures that will be used to obtain clients' informed consent for the release of confidential information and any exceptions to this

_____ Procedures for sharing information with colleagues for consultation, supervision, and coordination of services and why confidential information might be shared

_____ Solicitation of private information from clients

_____ Disclosure of confidential information to protect clients from self-harm and to protect third parties from harm

_____ Release of confidential information pertaining to alcohol and substance abuse treatment and services

_____ Disclosure of confidential information about deceased clients

47

_____ Release of confidential information to minor clients' parents or guardians

_____ Sharing of confidential information among parties in family, couples, marital, and group counseling

_____ Disclosure of confidential information to media representatives, law enforcement officials, protective services agencies, other social services agencies, and collection agencies

_____ Protection of confidential written and electronic records, information transmitted to other parties through the use of computers, electronic mail, facsimile machines, telephones and telephone answering machines, and other electronic or computer technology

_____ Transfer and disposal of clients' records

_____ Protection of client confidentiality in the event of the social worker's death, disability, or employment termination

_____ Precautions to prevent discussion of confidential information in public or semipublic areas

_____ Disclosure of confidential information to third-party payers

_____ Disclosure of confidential information to consultants

_____ Disclosure of confidential information when discussing clients for teaching or training purposes

_____ Protection of client confidentiality during legal proceedings

_____ Protection of client confidentiality during research and evaluation

_____ Providing staff with appropriate office space and meeting areas to ensure confidentiality and privacy

_____ Providing staff with appropriate office equipment and technology to ensure confidentiality and privacy (for example, secure file cabinets, wireless telephones, computer files, and facsimile machines)

Informed consent: The agency has appropriate policies and procedures in place to ensure proper informed consent.

POLICIES

1 point **no risk:** *clear, comprehensive policies exist concerning the following key aspects of informed consent, consistent with relevant laws, regulations, and ethical standards*

2 points **minimal risk:** *policies concerning informed consent exist, but require minor revision*

3 points **moderate risk:** *policies concerning informed consent exist, but require significant revision; policies concerning informed consent need to be created*

4 points **high risk:** *existing policies are inadequate or are seriously flawed; policies need to be created to address a significant number of informed consent issues*

_____ Absence of coercion and undue influence

_____ Assessment of client competence (for example, mental, language)

_____ Validity of consent forms (sufficient detail concerning purpose of consent, possible benefits, risks, costs, alternatives, and clients' right to refuse or withdraw consent; use of clear terminology; signature; and expiration dates)

_____ Proper verbal explanation of consent procedure

_____ Periodic renewal of clients' consent

_____ Appropriate use of translators and interpreters

_____ Exceptions to informed consent requirement

PROCEDURES

1 point **no risk:** *social workers routinely use proper procedures to obtain clients' informed consent, with specific regard to the following aspects of the informed consent process*

2 points **minimal risk:** *social workers usually use proper procedures to obtain clients' informed consent, but there are exceptions*

3 points **moderate risk:** *social workers are very inconsistent in their use of proper procedures to obtain clients' informed consent*

4 points **high risk:** *social workers rarely or never use proper procedures to obtain clients' informed consent*

_____ Absence of coercion and undue influence

_____ Assessment of client competence (for example, mental, language)

_____ Validity of consent forms (sufficient detail concerning purpose of consent, possible benefits, risks, costs, alternatives, and clients' right to refuse or withdraw consent; use of clear terminology; signature and expiration dates)

_____ Proper verbal explanation of consent procedure

_____ Periodic renewal of clients' consent

_____ Appropriate use of translators and interpreters

_____ Exceptions to informed consent requirement

Service delivery: The agency has appropriate policies and procedures in place to ensure proper delivery of services.

Staff Competence and Credentials

POLICIES

1 point **no risk:** *clear, comprehensive policies exist concerning staff competence and credentials (required skills, education, training, license, certification, consultation received; supervised experience; professional experience), consistent with relevant laws, regulations, and ethical standards*

2 points **minimal risk:** *policies concerning staff competence and credentials exist, but require minor revision*

3 points **moderate risk:** *policies concerning staff competence and credentials exist, but require significant revision; policies concerning some aspects of staff competence and credentials need to be created*

4 points **high risk:** *existing policies are inadequate or are seriously flawed; policies need to be created to address a significant number of issues concerning staff competence and credentials*

_____ Professional skills

_____ Professional education and training

_____ License and certification

_____ Consultation received

_____ Supervised experience

_____ Professional experience

PROCEDURES

1 point **no risk:** *social workers routinely use proper procedures to assess and ensure staff competence and credentials*

2 points **minimal risk:** *social workers usually use proper procedures to assess and ensure staff competence and credentials, but there are exceptions*

3 points **moderate risk:** *social workers are very inconsistent in their use of proper procedures to assess and ensure staff competence and credentials*

4 points **high risk:** *social workers rarely or never use proper procedures to assess and ensure staff competence and credentials*

_____ Professional skills

_____ Professional education and training

_____ License and certification

_____ Consultation received

_____ Supervised experience

_____ Professional experience

Use of Nontraditional or Experimental Interventions

POLICIES

1 point   no risk: *clear, comprehensive policies exist concerning social workers' use of nontraditional or experimental interventions, consistent with relevant laws, regulations, and ethical standards*

2 points   minimal risk: *policies concerning practitioners' use of nontraditional or experimental interventions exist, but require minor revision*

3 points   moderate risk: *policies concerning practitioners' use of nontraditional or experimental interventions exist, but require significant revision; policies concerning aspects of practitioners' use of nontraditional or experimental interventions need to be created*

4 points   high risk: *existing policies are inadequate or are seriously flawed; policies need to be created to address a significant number of issues related to practitioners' use of nontraditional or experimental interventions*

_____ Proper use of nontraditional or experimental interventions

_____ Appropriate consultation of professional literature (including research literature)

_____ Appropriate training

_____ Appropriate consultation with knowledgeable colleagues

_____ Appropriate use of supervision

PROCEDURES

1 point   no risk: *practitioners routinely follow proper procedures when using nontraditional or experimental interventions*

2 points   minimal risk: *practitioners usually follow proper procedures when using nontraditional or experimental interventions, but there are exceptions*

3 points   moderate risk: *practitioners are very inconsistent in their use of proper procedures when using nontraditional or experimental interventions*

4 points   high risk: *practitioners rarely or never follow proper procedures when using nontraditional or experimental interventions*

_____ Proper use of nontraditional or experimental interventions

_____ Appropriate consultation of professional literature (including research literature)

_____ Appropriate training

_____ Appropriate consultation with knowledgeable colleagues

_____ Appropriate use of supervision

Boundary issues and conflicts of interest: The agency has appropriate policies and procedures in place concerning employees' handling of boundary issues and conflicts of interest.

POLICIES

1 point   **no risk:** *clear, comprehensive policies exist concerning practitioners' handling of the following potential boundary issues and conflicts of interest, consistent with relevant laws, regulations, and ethical standards*

2 points   **minimal risk:** *policies concerning practitioners' handling of potential boundary issues and conflicts of interest exist, but require minor revision*

3 points   **moderate risk:** *policies concerning practitioners' handling of potential boundary issues and conflicts of interest exist, but require significant revision; policies concerning aspects of practitioners' handling of boundary issues and conflicts of interest need to be created*

4 points   **high risk:** *existing policies are inadequate or are seriously flawed; policies need to be created to address a significant number of issues related to practitioners' handling of boundary issues and conflicts of interest*

_____ Sexual relationships with current clients

_____ Sexual relationships with former clients

_____ Counseling of former sexual partners

_____ Sexual relationships with clients' relatives or acquaintances

_____ Sexual relationships with supervisees, trainees, students, and colleagues

_____ Physical contact with clients

_____ Friendships with current clients

_____ Friendships with former clients

_____ Encounters with clients in public settings

_____ Attendance at clients' social, religious, or lifecycle events

_____ Gifts from clients

_____ Gifts to clients

_____ Favors for clients

_____ Delivery of services in clients' homes

_____ Financial conflicts of interest

_____ Delivery of services to two or more people who have a relationship with each other

_____ Barter with clients for goods and services

_____ Relationships with clients in small or rural communities

_____ Self-disclosure to clients

_____ Collegial relationships with a former client

_____ Hiring of former clients

_____ Financial conflicts of interest for agency administrators or staff

_____ Financial conflicts of interest for members of agency governing bodies

PROCEDURES

1 point   **no risk:** *practitioners routinely follow proper procedures when they encounter boundary issues and conflicts of interest*

2 points   **minimal risk:** *practitioners usually follow proper procedures when they encounter boundary issues and conflicts of interest, but there are exceptions*

3 points   **moderate risk:** *practitioners are very inconsistent in their use of proper procedures to handle boundary issues and conflicts of interest*

4 points   **high risk:** *practitioners rarely or never follow proper procedures when they encounter boundary issues and conflicts of interest*

_____ Sexual relationships with current clients

_____ Sexual relationships with former clients

_____ Counseling of former sexual partners

_____ Sexual relationships with clients' relatives or acquaintances

_____ Sexual relationships with supervisees, trainees, students, and colleagues

_____ Physical contact with clients

_____ Friendships with current clients

_____ Friendships with former clients

_____ Encounters with clients in public settings

_____ Attendance at clients' social, religious, or lifecycle events

_____ Gifts from clients

_____ Gifts to clients

_____ Favors for clients

_____ Delivery of services in clients' homes

_____ Financial conflicts of interest

_____ Delivery of services to two or more people who have a relationship with each other

_____ Barter with clients for goods and services

_____ Relationships with clients in small or rural communities

_____ Self-disclosure to clients

_____ Collegial relationships with a former client

_____ Hiring of former clients

_____ Financial conflicts of interest for agency administrators or staff

_____ Financial conflicts of interest for members of agency governing bodies

Documentation: The agency has appropriate policies and procedures in place to ensure proper documentation.

POLICIES

1 point   **no risk:** *clear, comprehensive policies exist concerning practitioners' documentation in client records, consistent with relevant laws, regulations, and ethical standards*

2 points   **minimal risk:** *policies concerning practitioners' documentation in clients' records exist, but require minor revision*

3 points   **moderate risk:** *policies concerning practitioners' documentation in client records exist, but require significant revision; policies concerning aspects of practitioners' documentation in client records need to be created*

4 points   **high risk:** *existing policies are inadequate or are seriously flawed; policies need to be created to address a significant number of issues related to practitioners' documentation in clients' records*

_____ Social histories, assessments, and treatment plans

_____ Informed consent procedures

_____ Contacts with clients (type, date, time)

_____ Contacts with third parties

_____ Consultation with other professionals

_____ Decisions made and interventions/services provided

_____ Critical incidents

_____ Instructions, recommendations, advice, referrals to specialists

_____ Failed and canceled appointments

_____ Previous or current psychological, psychiatric, and medical evaluations

_____ Information concerning fees, charges, payments

_____ Termination of services

_____ Final assessment

_____ Inclusion of relevant documents (for example, consent forms, correspondence, court documents, fee agreements)

PROCEDURES

1 point **no risk:** *practitioners routinely follow proper procedures when they document in clients' records*

2 points **minimal risk:** *practitioners usually follow proper procedures when they document in clients' records, but there are exceptions*

3 points **moderate risk:** *practitioners are very inconsistent in their use of proper procedures when they document in clients' records*

4 points **high risk:** *practitioners rarely or never follow proper procedures concerning documentation in clients' records*

_____ Social histories, assessments, and treatment plans

_____ Informed consent procedures

_____ Contacts with clients (type, date, time)

_____ Contacts with third parties

_____ Consultation with other professionals

_____ Decisions made and interventions/services provided

_____ Critical incidents

_____ Instructions, recommendations, advice, referrals to specialists

_____ Failed and canceled appointments

_____ Previous or current psychological, psychiatric, and medical evaluations

_____ Information concerning fees, charges, payments

_____ Termination of services

_____ Final assessment

_____ Inclusion of relevant documents (for example, consent forms, correspondence, court documents, fee agreements)

Defamation of character: The agency has appropriate policies and procedures in place to prevent defamation of character.

POLICIES

1 point   **no risk:** *clear, comprehensive policies exist concerning practitioners' use of libelous or slanderous language in written and oral communication, consistent with relevant laws, regulations, and ethical standards*

2 points   **minimal risk:** *policies concerning practitioners' use of libelous or slanderous language exist, but require minor revision*

3 points   **moderate risk:** *policies concerning practitioners' use of libelous or slanderous language exist, but require significant revision; policies concerning aspects of practitioners' use of libelous or slanderous language need to be created*

4 points   **high risk:** *existing policies are inadequate or are seriously flawed; policies need to be created to address a significant number of issues related to practitioners' use of libelous or slanderous language*

_____ Libel (defamation that occurs in written form)

_____ Slander (defamation that occurs in oral form)

PROCEDURES

1 point   **no risk:** *practitioners routinely follow proper procedures to prevent defamation of character*

2 points   **minimal risk:** *practitioners usually follow proper procedures to prevent defamation of character, but there are exceptions*

3 points   **moderate risk:** *practitioners are very inconsistent in their use of proper procedures to prevent defamation of character*

4 points   **high risk:** *practitioners rarely or never follow proper procedures to prevent defamation of character*

_____ Libel (defamation that occurs in written form)

_____ Slander (defamation that occurs in oral form)

Client records: The agency has policies and procedures in place to ensure proper handling of client records.

POLICIES

1 point **no risk:** *clear, comprehensive policies exist concerning practitioners' handling of client records, consistent with relevant laws, regulations, and ethical standards*

2 points **minimal risk:** *policies concerning practitioners' handling of client records exist, but require minor revision*

3 points **moderate risk:** *policies concerning practitioners' handling of client records exist, but require significant revision; policies concerning aspects of practitioners' handling of client records need to be created*

4 points **high risk:** *existing policies are inadequate or are seriously flawed; policies need to be created to address a significant number of issues related to practitioners' handling of client records*

_____ Secure storage of records

_____ Proper retention of records

_____ Maintenance of records in the event of social worker's disability, incapacitation, termination of practice, or death

PROCEDURES

1 point **no risk:** *practitioners routinely follow proper procedures related to the handling of client records*

2 points **minimal risk:** *practitioners usually follow proper procedures related to the handling of client records, but there are exceptions*

3 points **moderate risk:** *practitioners are very inconsistent in their use of proper procedures related to the handling of client records*

4 points **high risk:** *practitioners rarely or never follow proper procedures related to the handling of client records*

_____ Secure storage of records

_____ Proper retention of records

_____ Maintenance of records in the event of social worker's disability, incapacitation, termination of practice, or death

57

Supervision: The agency has policies and procedures in place to ensure proper supervision of staff.

POLICIES

1 point **no risk:** *clear, comprehensive policies exist concerning staff supervision, consistent with relevant laws, regulations, and ethical standards*

2 points **minimal risk:** *policies concerning staff supervision exist, but require minor revision*

3 points **moderate risk:** *policies concerning staff supervision exist, but require significant revision; policies concerning aspects of staff supervision need to be created*

4 points **high risk:** *existing policies are inadequate or are seriously flawed; policies need to be created to address a significant number of issues related to staff supervision*

_____ Supervisors provide information necessary for supervisees to obtain clients' informed consent

_____ Supervisors oversee supervisees' efforts to develop and implement thorough treatment and intervention plans

_____ Supervisors identify and respond to supervisees' errors in all phases of client contact, such as the inappropriate disclosure of confidential information

_____ Supervisors know when supervisees' clients need to be reassigned, transferred, or have their treatment terminated

_____ Supervisors know when supervisees should arrange for consultation

_____ Supervisors monitor supervisees' competence and willingness to address incompetence, impairment, and unethical behavior

_____ Supervisors monitor proper boundaries between supervisees and their clients

_____ Supervisors protect third parties from physical harm

_____ Supervisors detect or stop a negligent treatment plan or treatment carried out longer than necessary

_____ Supervisors determine that a specialist is needed for treatment of a particular client

_____ Supervisors meet regularly with the supervisees

_____ Supervisors review and approve the supervisees' records, decisions, and actions

_____ Supervisors provide adequate coverage in a supervisee's absence

_____ Supervisors document supervision provided

_____ Supervisors maintain proper boundaries in relationships with supervisees

_____ Supervisors provide supervisees with timely and informative performance evaluations and feedback

_____ Supervisors prepare written supervision agreements

_____ Supervisors are receptive to supervisees' efforts to raise ethical concerns and issues

_____ Supervisors provide supervisees with sufficient time and appropriate workloads to enable them to meet their professional responsibilities

_____ Supervisors have sufficient time in their workloads to provide proper supervision

PROCEDURES

1 point   **no risk:** *practitioners routinely follow proper staff supervision procedures*

2 points   **minimal risk:** *practitioners usually follow staff supervision procedures, but there are exceptions*

3 points   **moderate risk:** *practitioners are very inconsistent in their use of staff supervision procedures*

4 points   **high risk:** *practitioners rarely or never follow staff supervision procedures*

_____ Supervisors provide information necessary for supervisees to obtain clients' informed consent

_____ Supervisors oversee supervisees' efforts to develop and implement thorough treatment and intervention plans

_____ Supervisors identify and respond to supervisees' errors in all phases of client contact, such as the inappropriate disclosure of confidential information

_____ Supervisors know when supervisees' clients need to be reassigned, transferred, or have their treatment terminated

_____ Supervisors know when supervisees should arrange for consultation

_____ Supervisors monitor supervisees' competence and willingness to address incompetence, impairment, and unethical behavior

_____ Supervisors monitor proper boundaries between supervisees and their clients

_____ Supervisors protect third parties from physical harm

_____ Supervisors detect or stop a negligent treatment plan or treatment carried out longer than necessary

_____ Supervisors determine that a specialist is needed for treatment of a particular client

_____ Supervisors meet regularly with the supervisees

_____ Supervisors review and approve the supervisees' records, decisions, and actions

_____ Supervisors provide adequate coverage in a supervisee's absence

_____ Supervisors document supervision provided

_____ Supervisors maintain proper boundaries in relationships with supervisees

_____ Supervisors provide supervisees with timely and informative performance evaluations and feedback

_____ Supervisors prepare written supervision agreements

_____ Supervisors are receptive to supervisees' efforts to raise ethical concerns and issues

_____ Supervisors provide supervisees with sufficient time and appropriate workloads to enable them to meet their professional responsibilities

_____ Supervisors have sufficient time in their workloads to provide proper supervision

Staff development and training: The agency has policies and procedures in place to ensure that staff have appropriate training.

POLICIES

1 point **no risk:** *clear, comprehensive policies exist concerning staff training on critical topics, consistent with relevant laws, regulations, and ethical standards*

2 points **minimal risk:** *policies concerning staff training exist, but require minor revision*

3 points **moderate risk:** *policies concerning staff training exist, but require significant revision; policies concerning aspects of staff training need to be created*

4 points **high risk:** *existing policies are inadequate or are seriously flawed; policies need to be created to address a significant number of issues related to staff training*

_____ Relevant practice skills

_____ Professional ethics and liability (especially major risk areas and steps to take when making ethical decisions)

_____ Relevant federal, state, and local statutes and regulations

_____ Assessment tools

_____ Intervention techniques

_____ Evaluation methods

_____ Emergency assistance and suicide prevention

_____ Supervision of clients in residential programs

_____ Confidentiality and privileged communication

_____ Informed consent

_____ Improper treatment and service delivery

_____ Defamation of character

_____ Boundary issues in relationships with clients and colleagues (dual and multiple relationships)

_____ Consultation with and referral to colleagues and specialists

_____ Fraud and deception

_____ Termination of services

PROCEDURES

1 point **no risk:** *administrators and supervisors routinely follow proper procedures related to staff training on key topics*

2 points **minimal risk:** *administrators and supervisors usually follow proper procedures related to staff training, but there are exceptions*

3 points **moderate risk:** *administrators and supervisors are very inconsistent in their use of proper procedures related to staff training*

4 points **high risk:** *administrators and supervisors rarely or never follow proper procedures related to staff training*

_____ Relevant practice skills

_____ Professional ethics and liability (especially major risk areas and steps to take when making ethical decisions)

_____ Relevant federal, state, and local statutes and regulations

_____ Assessment tools

_____ Intervention techniques

_____ Evaluation methods

_____ Emergency assistance and suicide prevention

_____ Supervision of clients in residential programs

_____ Confidentiality and privileged communication

_____ Informed consent

_____ Improper treatment and service delivery

_____ Defamation of character

_____ Boundary issues in relationships with clients and colleagues (dual and multiple relationships)

_____ Consultation with and referral to colleagues and specialists

_____ Fraud and deception

_____ Termination of services

Consultation: The agency has policies and procedures in place to ensure that staff seek proper consultation.

POLICIES

1 point   **no risk:** *clear, comprehensive policies exist concerning staff use of consultants, consistent with relevant laws, regulations, and ethical standards*

2 points **minimal risk:** *policies concerning staff consultation exist, but require minor revision*

3 points **moderate risk:** *policies concerning staff consultation exist, but require significant revision; policies concerning aspects of staff consultation need to be created*

4 points **high risk:** *existing policies are inadequate or are seriously flawed; policies need to be created to address a significant number of issues related to staff consultation*

_____ Staff use consultants when necessary

_____ Staff screen consultants to ensure competence

PROCEDURES

1 point   **no risk:** *staff routinely follow proper procedures related to their use of consultants*

2 points **minimal risk:** *staff usually follow proper procedures related to their use of consultants, but there are exceptions*

3 points **moderate risk:** *staff are very inconsistent in their use of proper procedures to obtain consultation*

4 points **high risk:** *staff rarely or never follow proper procedures related to use of consultants*

_____ Staff use consultants when necessary

_____ Staff screen consultants to ensure competence

Client referral: The agency has appropriate policies and procedures in place to ensure that staff refer clients to other service providers when necessary.

POLICIES

1 point **no risk:** *clear, comprehensive policies exist concerning referral of clients to other service providers, consistent with relevant laws, regulations, and ethical standards*

2 points **minimal risk:** *policies concerning referral of clients to other service providers exist, but require minor revision*

3 points **moderate risk:** *policies concerning referral of clients to other service providers exist but require significant revision; policies concerning aspects of client referral need to be created*

4 points **high risk:** *existing policies are inadequate or are seriously flawed; policies need to be created to address a significant number of issues related to client referral*

_____ Staff refer clients to specialists when necessary

_____ Staff screen specialists for client referral to ensure competence

_____ Staff monitor referrals (follow-up)

PROCEDURES

1 point **no risk:** *staff routinely follow proper procedures related to their referral of clients to other service providers*

2 points **minimal risk:** *staff usually follow proper procedures related to their referral of clients to other service providers, but there are exceptions*

3 points **moderate risk:** *staff are very inconsistent in their use of proper procedures to refer clients*

4 points **high risk:** *staff rarely or never follow proper procedures related to client referral*

_____ Staff refer clients to specialists when necessary

_____ Staff screen specialists for client referral to ensure competence

_____ Staff monitor referrals (follow-up)

Fraud: The agency has appropriate policies and procedures in place to prevent fraud.

POLICIES

1 point   **no risk:** *clear, comprehensive policies exist concerning fraud prevention, consistent with relevant laws, regulations, and ethical standards*

2 points   **minimal risk:** *policies concerning fraud prevention exist, but require minor revision*

3 points   **moderate risk:** *policies concerning fraud prevention exist, but require significant revision; policies concerning aspects of fraud prevention need to be created*

4 points   **high risk:** *existing policies are inadequate or are seriously flawed; policies need to be created to address a significant number of issues related to fraud prevention*

_____ Documentation in client records (for example, client contacts, services provided)

_____ Billing

_____ Personnel records (for example, employment applications, expense vouchers, personal leave requests)

PROCEDURES

1 point   **no risk:** *staff routinely follow proper procedures related to fraud prevention*

2 points   **minimal risk:** *staff usually follow proper procedures related to fraud prevention, but there are exceptions*

3 points   **moderate risk:** *staff are very inconsistent in their use of proper procedures to prevent fraud*

4 points   **high risk:** *staff rarely or never follow proper procedures related to fraud prevention*

_____ Documentation in client records (for example, client contacts, services provided)

_____ Billing

_____ Personnel records (for example, employment applications, expense vouchers, personal leave requests)

Termination of services and client abandonment: The agency has policies and procedures in place to ensure proper termination of services.

POLICIES

1 point   **no risk:** *clear, comprehensive policies exist concerning termination of services to clients, consistent with relevant laws, regulations, and ethical standards*

2 points   **minimal risk:** *policies concerning termination of services exist, but require minor revision*

3 points   **moderate risk:** *policies concerning termination of services exist, but require significant revision; policies concerning aspects of service termination need to be created*

4 points   **high risk:** *existing policies are inadequate or are seriously flawed; policies need to be created to address a significant number of issues related to termination of services*

_____ Termination of services as a result of employee departure

_____ Termination of services as a result of client nonpayment of an outstanding balance

_____ Termination of services as a result of client noncompliance

_____ Notification of terminated clients

_____ Documentation of decisions and actions concerning termination of services

_____ Delivery of services in emergency circumstances

PROCEDURES

1 point   **no risk:** *staff routinely follow proper procedures related to termination of services*

2 points   **minimal risk:** *staff usually follow proper procedures related to termination of services, but there are exceptions*

3 points   **moderate risk:** *staff are very inconsistent in their use of proper procedures to terminate services*

4 points   **high risk:** *staff rarely or never follow proper procedures related to service termination*

_____ Termination of services as a result of employee departure

_____ Termination of services as a result of client nonpayment of an outstanding balance

_____ Termination of services as a result of client noncompliance

_____ Notification of terminated clients

_____ Documentation of decisions and actions concerning termination of services

_____ Delivery of services in emergency circumstances

Practitioner impairment: The agency has appropriate policies and procedures in place to address practitioner impairment.

POLICIES

1 point **no risk:** *clear, comprehensive policies exist concerning practitioner impairment, consistent with relevant laws, regulations, and ethical standards*

2 points **minimal risk:** *policies concerning practitioner impairment exist, but require minor revision*

3 points **moderate risk:** *policies concerning practitioner impairment exist, but require significant revision; policies concerning aspects of practitioner impairment need to be created*

4 points **high risk:** *existing policies are inadequate or are seriously flawed; policies need to be created to address a significant number of issues related to practitioner impairment*

_____ Staff familiarity with the nature, causes, and signs of impairment

_____ Staff use of strategies to address colleagues' impairment

_____ Staff use of strategies to address practitioners' own impairment

PROCEDURES

1 point **no risk:** *staff routinely follow proper procedures related to practitioner impairment*

2 points **minimal risk:** *staff usually follow proper procedures related to practitioner impairment, but there are exceptions*

3 points **moderate risk:** *staff are very inconsistent in their use of proper procedures related to practitioner impairment*

4 points **high risk:** *staff rarely or never follow proper procedures related to practitioner impairment*

_____ Staff familiarity with the nature, causes, and signs of impairment

_____ Staff use of strategies to address colleagues' impairment

_____ Staff use of strategies to address practitioners' own impairment

Evaluation and research: The agency has appropriate policies and procedures in place to monitor and evaluate services, policies, and programs, and to protect evaluation and research participants.

POLICIES

1 point **no risk:** *clear, comprehensive policies exist concerning evaluation and research—including the protection of evaluation and research participants—consistent with relevant laws, regulations, and ethical standards*

2 points **minimal risk:** *policies concerning evaluation and research exist, but require minor revision*

3 points **moderate risk:** *policies concerning evaluation and research exist, but require significant revision; policies concerning aspects of evaluation and research need to be created*

4 points **high risk:** *existing policies are inadequate or are seriously flawed; policies need to be created to address a significant number of issues related to evaluation and research*

_____ Conduct research and evaluate programs, policies, and services

_____ Keep current with emerging knowledge relevant to social work, and use evaluation and research evidence in professional practice

_____ Follow guidelines developed for the protection of evaluation and research participants (including consultation of appropriate institutional review boards)

_____ Obtain voluntary and written informed consent from evaluation and research participants, when appropriate

_____ Inform participants of their right to withdraw from evaluation and research at any time without penalty

_____ Take appropriate steps to ensure that participants in evaluation and research have access to appropriate supportive services

_____ Protect evaluation and research participants from unwarranted physical or mental distress, harm, danger, or deprivation

_____ Discuss collected information only for professional purposes and only with people professionally concerned with this information

_____ Ensure the anonymity or confidentiality of participants and of the data obtained from them, to the extent permitted by law and regulation

_____ Protect research and evaluation participants' confidentiality by omitting identifying information unless proper consent has been obtained authorizing disclosure

_____ Report evaluation and research findings accurately

_____ Avoid conflicts of interest and dual relationships with evaluation and research participants

PROCEDURES

    1 point   **no risk:** *staff routinely follow proper procedures related to evaluation and research*

    2 points **minimal risk:** *staff usually follow proper procedures related to evaluation and research, but there are exceptions*

    3 points **moderate risk:** *staff are very inconsistent in their use of proper procedures related to evaluation and research*

    4 points **high risk:** *staff rarely or never follow proper procedures related to evaluation and research*

_____ Conduct research and evaluate programs, policies, and services

_____ Keep current with emerging knowledge relevant to social work, and use evaluation and research evidence in professional practice

_____ Follow guidelines developed for the protection of evaluation and research participants (including consultation of appropriate institutional review boards)

_____ Obtain voluntary and written informed consent from evaluation and research participants, when appropriate

_____ Inform participants of their right to withdraw from evaluation and research at any time without penalty

_____ Take appropriate steps to ensure that participants in evaluation and research have access to appropriate supportive services

_____ Protect evaluation and research participants from unwarranted physical or mental distress, harm, danger, or deprivation

_____ Discuss collected information only for professional purposes and only with people professionally concerned with this information

_____ Ensure the anonymity or confidentiality of participants and of the data obtained from them, to the extent permitted by law and regulation

_____ Protect research and evaluation participants' confidentiality by omitting identifying information unless proper consent has been obtained authorizing disclosure

_____ Report evaluation and research findings accurately

_____ Avoid conflicts of interest and dual relationships with evaluation and research participants

Ethical decision making: The agency has appropriate policies and procedures in place to ensure sound ethical decisions.

POLICIES

1 point   **no risk:** *clear, comprehensive policies exist concerning staff use of ethical decision-making protocols, consistent with current knowledge and relevant ethical standards*

2 points   **minimal risk:** *policies concerning staff use of ethical decision-making protocols exist, but require minor revision*

3 points   **moderate risk:** *policies concerning staff use of ethical decision-making protocols exist, but require significant revision; policies concerning aspects of ethical decision making need to be created*

4 points   **high risk:** *existing policies are inadequate or are seriously flawed; policies need to be created to address a significant number of issues related to ethical decision making*

_____ Staff ability to recognize ethical dilemmas

_____ Staff familiarity with and ability to use ethical decision-making protocols

_____ Staff familiarity with and ability to use:

  Ethical theory, principles, and guidelines

  Codes of ethics (especially the NASW *Code of Ethics*)

  Legal principles (including relevant laws, regulations, and court decisions)

  Ethics consultation (agency staff, supervisors, administrators, ethics experts, ethics committees)

_____ Documentation of ethical decisions

_____ Monitoring and evaluation of ethical decisions

PROCEDURES

1 point   **no risk:** *staff routinely follow proper procedures related to ethical decision making*

2 points   **minimal risk:** *staff usually follow proper procedures when making ethical decisions, but there are exceptions*

3 points   **moderate risk:** *staff are very inconsistent in their use of proper procedures related to ethical decisions*

4 points   **high risk:** *staff rarely or never follow proper procedures related to ethical decisions*

_____ Staff ability to recognize ethical dilemmas

_____ Staff familiarity with and ability to use ethical decision-making protocols

_____ Staff familiarity with and ability to use:

  Ethical theory, principles, and guidelines

  Codes of ethics (especially the NASW *Code of Ethics*)

  Legal principles (including relevant laws, regulations, and court decisions)

  Ethics consultation (agency staff, supervisors, administrators, ethics experts, ethics committees)

_____ Documentation of ethical decisions

_____ Monitoring and evaluation of ethical decisions

Part II: Action Plan

1 Risk area:

_____

2 Risk level:

☐ High risk   ☐ Moderate risk   ☐ Minimal risk

3 Summary of steps required to reduce risk:

_____
_____
_____
_____

4 Agency resources required (for example, personnel, publications, appointment of committee or task force, legal consultation, ethics consultation, staff development time):

_____
_____
_____
_____

5 Personnel responsible for overseeing implementation of Action Plan:

_____
_____
_____

6 Timetable for completion of Action Plan (key beginning and ending dates for individual tasks):

_____
_____
_____

7 Indicators of progress toward minimizing risk (for example, revision of specific documents, staff development and training on specific topics):

_____
_____
_____

8 Plans to monitor implementation of the Action Plan:

_____
_____
_____
_____

REFERENCES

Alexander, R., Jr. (1997). Social workers and privileged communication in the federal legal system. *Social Work, 42,* 387–391.

Applebaum, P.S., Lidz, C.W., & Meisel, A. (1987). *Informed consent: Legal theory and clinical practice.* New York: Oxford University Press.

Austin, K.M., Moline, M.E., & Williams, G.T. (1990). *Confronting malpractice: Legal and ethical dilemmas in psychotherapy.* Newbury Park, CA: Sage.

Barker, R.L., & Branson, D.M. (2000). *Forensic social work* (2nd ed.). New York: Haworth Press.

Berliner, A.K. (1989). Misconduct in social work practice. *Social Work, 34,* 69–72.

Bernstein, B., & Hartsell, T. (1998). *The portable lawyer for mental health professionals.* New York: John Wiley & Sons.

Bernstein, B., & Hartsell, T. (2000). *The portable ethicist for mental health professionals.* New York: John Wiley & Sons.

Besharov, D. (1985). *The vulnerable social worker.* Silver Spring, MD: National Association of Social Workers.

Bissell, L., & Haberman, P.W. (1984). *Alcoholism in the professions.* New York: Oxford University Press.

Bullis, R.K. (1995). *Clinical social worker misconduct.* Chicago: Nelson-Hall.

Callahan, D., & Bok, S. (1980). *Ethics teaching in higher education.* New York: Plenum.

Cohen, R.J., & Mariano, W.E. (1982). *Legal guidebook in mental health.* New York: Free Press.

Congress, E.P. (1998). *Social work values and ethics.* Chicago: Nelson-Hall.

Conrad, A.P. (1989). Developing an ethics review process in a social service agency. *Social Thought, 15,* 102–115.

Courtemanche, G. (1989). *Audit management and supervision.* New York: John Wiley & Sons.

Cowles, J.K. (1976). *Informed consent.* New York: Coward, McCann, and Geoghegan.

Dean, R.G., & Rhodes, M. (1992). Ethical-clinical tensions in clinical practice. *Social Work, 39*(2), 128–132.

Dickson, D.T. (1995). *Law in the health and human services.* New York: Free Press.

Dickson, D.T. (1998). *Confidentiality and privacy in social work.* New York: Free Press.

Dworkin, G. (1971). Paternalism. In R.A. Wasserstrom (Ed.), *Morality and the law* (pp. 107–126). Belmont, CA: Wadsworth.

71

Epstein, R. (1994). *Keeping boundaries.* Washington, DC: American Psychiatric Press.

Fausel, D.F. (1988). Helping the helper heal: Co-dependency in helping professionals. *Journal of Independent Social Work, 3*(2), 35–45.

Foster, L.W. (1995). Bioethical issues. In R. L. Edwards (Ed.-in-Chief), *Encyclopedia of social work* (19th ed., Vol. 1, pp. 292–298). Washington, DC: NASW Press.

Frankena, W.K. (1973). *Ethics* (2nd ed.). Englewood Cliffs, NJ: Prentice Hall.

Gambrill, E., & Pruger, R. (Eds.). (1997). *Controversial issues in social work: Ethics, values, and obligations.* Needham Heights, MA: Allyn & Bacon.

Gifis, S.H. (Ed.). (1991). *Law dictionary* (3rd ed.). Hauppauge, NY: Barron's.

Grinnell, R.M., Jr. (Ed.) (1997). *Social work research and evaluation* (5th ed.). Itasca, IL: F. E. Peacock.

Grossman, M. (1978). Confidentiality: The right to privacy versus the right to know. In W. E. Barton & C. J. Sanborn (Eds.), *Law and the mental health professions* (p. 137). New York: International Universities Press.

Gutheil, T., & Gabbard, G. (1993). The concept of boundaries in clinical practice: Theoretical and risk management dimensions. *American Journal of Psychiatry 150*(2), 188-196.

Guy, J.D., Poelstra, P.L., & Stark, M. (1989). Personal distress and therapeutic effectiveness: National survey of psychologists practicing psychotherapy. *Professional Psychology: Research and Practice, 20,* 48–50.

Haas, L.J., & Malouf, J.L. (1995). *Keeping up the good work: A practitioner's guide to mental health ethics* (2nd ed.). Sarasota, FL: Professional Resource Press.

Hancock, R.N. (1974). *Twentieth-century ethics.* New York: Columbia University Press.

Herlihy, B., & Corey, G. (1997). *Boundary issues in counseling: Multiple roles and responsibilities.* Alexandria, VA: American Counseling Association.

Hogan, D.B. (1979). *The regulation of psychotherapists. Vol. 1: A study in the philosophy and practice of professional regulation.* Cambridge, MA: Ballinger.

Houston-Vega, M.K., Nuehring, E.M., & Daguio, E.R. (1997). *Prudent practice: A guide for managing malpractice risk.* Washington, DC: NASW Press.

Jaffe v. Redmond, 116 S. Ct. 1923 (1996).

Jayaratne, S., Croxton, T., & Mattison, D. (1997). Social work professional standards: An exploratory study. *Social Work, 42,* 187–98.

Joseph, M.V. (1985). A model for ethical decision making in clinical practice. In C.B. Germain (Ed.), *Advances in clinical practice* (pp. 207–217). Silver Spring, MD: National Association of Social Workers.

Joseph, M.V. (1989). Social work ethics: Historical and contemporary perspectives. *Social Thought, 15,* 4–17.

Kagle, J.D. (1991). *Social work records* (3rd ed.). Belmont, CA: Wadsworth.

Kagle, J.D. (1995). Recording. In R.L. Edwards (Ed.-in-Chief), *Encyclopedia of social work* (19th ed., Vol. 3, pp. 2027–2033). Washington, DC: NASW Press.

Kagle, J.D., & Giebelhausen, P.N. (1994). Dual relationships and professional boundaries. *Social Work, 39,* 213–220.

Kirk, S., & Kutchins, H. (1988). Deliberate misdiagnosis in mental health. *Social Service Review, 62,* 225–237.

Kurzman, P.A. (1983). Ethical issues in industrial social work practice. *Social Casework, 64,* 105–111.

Lamb, D.H., Presser, N.R., Pfost, K.S., Baum, M.C., Jackson, V.R., & Jarvis, P.A. (1987). Confronting professional impairment during the internship: Identification, due process, and remediation. *Professional Psychology: Research and Practice, 18,* 597-603.

Levy, C.S. (1982). *Guide to ethical decisions and actions for social service administrators.* New York: Haworth Press.

Loewenberg, F., & Dolgoff, R. (1996). *Ethical decisions for social work practice* (5th ed.). Itasca, IL: F.E. Peacock.

Madden, R.G. (1998). *Legal issues in social work, counseling, and mental health.* Thousand Oaks, CA: Sage.

Meyer, R.G., Landis, E.R., & Hays, J.R. (1988). *Law for the psychotherapist.* New York: W.W. Norton.

National Association of Social Workers. (1994). *Guidelines for clinical social work supervision.* Washington, DC: Author.

National Association of Social Workers. (1996). *NASW Code of Ethics.* Washington, DC: Author.

Polowy, C.I., & Gorenberg, C. (1997). *Client confidentiality and privileged communications: Office of General Counsel law notes.* Washington, DC: National Association of Social Workers.

President's Commission for the Study of Ethical Problems in Medicine and Biomedical and Behavioral Research. (1982). *Making health care decisions: The ethical and legal implications of informed consent in the patient-practitioner relationship* (Vol. 3). Washington, DC: U.S. Government Printing Office.

Rachels, J. (1993). *The elements of moral philosophy* (2nd ed.). New York: McGraw-Hill.

Random House Webster's college dictionary (1991). New York: Random House.

Reamer, F.G. (1983). The concept of paternalism in social work. *Social Service Review 57*, 254–271.

Reamer, F.G. (1987a). Informed consent in social work. *Social Work, 32*, 425–429.

Reamer, F.G. (1987b). Ethics committees in social work. *Social Work, 32*, 188–92.

Reamer, F.G. (1989). Liability issues in social work supervision. *Social Work, 34*, 445–448.

Reamer, F.G. (1990). *Ethical dilemmas in social service* (2nd ed.). New York: Columbia University Press.

Reamer, F.G. (1992). The impaired social worker. *Social Work, 37*, 165–70.

Reamer, F.G. (1993). *The philosophical foundations of social work*. New York: Columbia University Press.

Reamer, F.G. (1994). *Social work malpractice and liability*. New York: Columbia University Press.

Reamer, F.G. (1997). Managing ethics under managed care. *Families in Society, 78*, 96–101.

Reamer, F.G. (1998). *Ethical standards in social work: A review of the NASW Code of Ethics*. Washington, DC: NASW Press.

Reamer, F.G. (1999). *Social work values and ethics* (2nd ed.). New York: Columbia University Press.

Reamer, F.G. (2001) *Tangled relationships: Managing boundary issues in the human services*. New York: Columbia University Press.

Reamer, F.G. (in press). Boundary issues in social work: Managing dual relationships. *Social Work*.

Rhodes, M. (1986). *Ethical dilemmas in social work practice*. London: Routledge & Kegan Paul.

Ross, W.D. (1930). *The right and the good*. Oxford, England: Clarendon.

Rozovsky, F.A. (1984). *Consent to treatment: A practical guide*. Boston: Little, Brown.

Rubin, A., & Babbie, E. (1997). *Research methods for social work* (3rd ed.). Pacific Grove, CA: Brooks/Cole.

Russell, J.P., & Regel, T. (1996). *After the quality audit: Closing the loop on the audit process*. Milwaukee, WI: ASQC Quality Press.

Schamess, G., & Lightburn, A. (Eds.) (1998). *Humane managed care?* Washington, DC: NASW Press.

Schoener, G.R., & Gonsiorek, J. (1988). Assessment and development of rehabilitation plans for counselors who have sexually exploited their clients. *Journal of Counseling and Development, 67*, 227–232.

Schutz, B.M. (1982). *Legal liability in psychotherapy*. San Francisco: Jossey-Bass.

Simon, R. (1999). Therapist-patient sex: From boundary violations to sexual misconduct. *Psychiatric Clinics of North America 22*(1), 31–47.

Sonnenstuhl, W.J. (1989). Reaching the impaired professional: Applying findings from organizational and occupational research. *Journal of Drug Issues, 19*, 533–539.

Strom-Gottfried, K. (1998). Is "ethical managed care" an oxymoron? *Families in Society, 79*, 297–307.

Tarasoff v. Board of Regents of the University of California, 33 Cal. 3d 275 (1973), 529 P. 2d 553 (1974), 17 Cal. 3d 425 (1976), 551 P. 2d 334 (1976), 131 Cal. Rptr. 14 (1976).

Thoreson, R.W., Miller, M., & Krauskopf, C.J. (1989). The distressed psychologist: Prevalence and treatment considerations. *Professional Psychology: Research and Practice, 20*, 153–158.

Tomes, J.P. (1993). *Informed consent: A guide for the healthcare professional*. Chicago: Probus Publishing Co.

VandenBos, G.R., & Duthie, R.F. (1986). Confronting and supporting colleagues in distress. In R.R. Kilburg, P.E. Nathan, & R.W. Thoreson (Eds.), *Professionals in distress: Issues, syndromes, and solutions in psychology* (p. 211). Washington, DC: American Psychological Association.

White, B. (1994). *Competence to consent*. Washington, DC: Georgetown University Press.

Wilson, S.J. (1978). *Confidentiality in social work*. New York: Free Press.

Wilson, S.J. (1980). *Recording: Guidelines for social workers* (2nd ed.). New York: Free Press.

Woody, R.H. (1997). *Legally safe mental health practice*. Madison, CT: Psychosocial Press.

INDEX

Book design: Weber Design, Alexandria, Virginia
Typefaces: Goudy and Frutiger
Printed by Graphic Communications Inc.

ESSENTIAL NASW PRESS TOOLS FOR ETHICAL SOCIAL WORK PRACTICE

The Social Work Ethics Audit: *A Risk Management Tool,* Frederic G. Reamer. *The Social Work Ethics Audit* provides practitioners with an easy-to-use tool that helps assess the adequacy of ethics-related policies, practices, and procedures related to clients, staff, documentation, and decision making. Designed to work seamlessly with the audit instrument and computer disk, the accompanying volume assists respondents in determining appropriate action steps and strategy to correct any inadequacies or lapses in ethical practices. It creates opportunity for intense self-evaluation and implementation of corrective measures for improved social work practice.
ISBN: 0-87101-328-2. Item #3282: Book with Word for Windows disk; Item #3282A: Book with Macintosh disk. March 2001. $39.99.

Current Controversies in Social Work Ethics: *Case Examples,* by NASW Code of Ethics Revision Committee, Frederic G. Reamer, Chairperson. Presents a cross-section of real examples of ethics dilemmas faced by social workers in contemporary practice situations. A companion work to the NASW *Code of Ethics,* this practical and thought-provoking handbook offers commentaries of related considerations and implications that help the reader untangle the controversies and competing values associated with ethical decision-making.
6" x 9" pamphlet. Item #3002. 100 pages. 1998. $8.50.

Ethical Standards in Social Work: *A Review of the NASW Code of Ethics,* by Frederic G. Reamer. Each section of the 1998 NASW *Code of Ethics* is analyzed in this volume with guidance for practice in areas such as confidentiality, boundary issues, informed consent, conflicts of interest, research and evaluation, and more.
ISBN: 0-87101-293-6. Item #2936. 308 pages. 1998. $24.95.

Prudent Practice: A Guide for Managing Malpractice Risk, *by Mary Kay Houston-Vega and Elane M. Nuehring with Elisabeth R. Daguio.* Social workers and other human service professionals face a heightened risk of malpractice suits in today's litigious society. The NASW Press offers practitioners a complete practice guide to increasing competence and managing the risk of malpractice. Included in the book and on disk are 25 sample forms and 5 sample fact sheets to distribute to clients.
ISBN: 0-87101-267-7. Item #2677: Book with Word for Windows disk; Item# 2677: Book with Macintosh disk, Item #2677A. 332 pages. 1996. $42.95.

The Legal Environment of Social Work, *by Leila Obier Schroeder.* This book focuses on the legal system as it influences the social work profession and highlights the laws that affect the delivery of social work services. Covers the criminal justice system, juvenile courts, marriage, filiation and adoption concerns, and legislation such as the American with Disabilities Act.
ISBN: 0-87101-235-9. Item #2359. 382 pages. 1995. $34.95.

Are Ethics and Contemporary Social Work Practice Compatible? (A self-study CEU product). During this information-packed 3-hour presentation, learn from social workers who practice in a variety of settings and hold differing viewpoints as they tackle some of the most compelling ethical issues facing contemporary social work practice—managed care, cultural competency, worker-client boundaries, risk management, and ethical decision making in agency settings.
Videotape. Item #V14. 2.5 hours. VHS 1/2". $69.00.

(Order form and information on reverse side)

ORDER FORM

Qty.	Title	Item #	Price	Total
___	The Social Work Ethics Audit			
___	Book with Word for Windows disk	3282	$39.99	_____
___	Book with Macintosh disk	3282A	$39.99	_____
___	Current Controversies in SW Ethics	3002	$8.50	_____
___	Ethical Standards in SW	2936	$24.95	_____
___	Prudent Practice			
___	Book with Word for Windows disk	2677	$42.95	_____
___	Book with Macintosh disk	2677A	$42.95	_____
___	Legal Environment of Social Work	2359	$34.95	_____
___	Are Ethics and Contemporary SW Practice Compatible?	V14	$69.00	_____

POSTAGE AND HANDLING
Minimum postage and handling fee is $4.95.
Orders that do not include appropriate postage
and handling will be returned.

DOMESTIC: Please add 12% to orders under $100
for postage and handling. For orders over $100
add 7% of order.

CANADA: Please add 17% postage and handling.

OTHER INTERNATIONAL: Please add 22% postage and
handling.

Subtotal	_____
Postage and Handling	_____
DC residents add 6% sales tax	_____
MD residents add 5% sales tax	_____
Total	_____

❑ **Check** or **money order** (payable to NASW Press) for $ _____.

❑ **Credit card**
   ❑ NASW Visa* | ❑ Visa | ❑ NASW MasterCard* | ❑ MasterCard | ❑ Amex

_____   _____
Credit Card Number   Expiration Date

Signature _____

Use of these cards generates funds in support of the social work profession.

Name _____

Address _____

City _____ State/Province _____

Country _____ Zip _____

Phone _____ E-mail _____

NASW Member # (if applicable) _____

(Please make checks payable to NASW Press. Prices are subject to change.)

NASW PRESS
P. O. Box 431
Annapolis JCT, MD 20701
USA

Credit card orders call
1-800-227-3590
(In the Metro Wash., DC, area, call 301-317-8688)
Or fax your order to 301-206-7989
Or order online at http://www.naswpress.org

Visit our Web site at http://www.naswpress.org.   3282BC